Collins need to know?

Birdwatching

Collins need to know?

Birdwatching

All the tips and techniques
you need to get into birdwatching

Rob Hume

First published in 2005 by
Collins, an imprint of
HarperCollins*Publishers*
77–85 Fulham Palace Road
Hammersmith, London W6 8JB

The Collins website address is:
www.collins.co.uk

Collins is a registered trademark of HarperCollins Publishers Limited.

09 08 07
6 5 4 3 2 1

The information contained in this book, including addresses, telephone numbers and website details, is correct at the time of going to press, but the publisher cannot accept responsibility for any subsequent changes.

A catalogue record for this book is available from the British Library

Created by: SP Creative Design
Editor: Heather Thomas
Designer: Sarah Crouch
Cover design: Cook Design
Photographs: rspb-images.com (see p. 190); HarperCollins Publishers: pp. 15, 26, 31
Front cover photograph: Malcolm Hunt/rspb-images.com
Back cover photographs: (top) Mark Hamblin/rspb-images.com;
(centre) Bob Glover/rspb-images.com; (bottom) Niall Benvie/rspb-images.com
Illustrations: Lizzie Harper: pp. 45, 47

ISBN-13 978 0 00 779354 9

Colour reproduction by Colourscan, Singapore
Printed and bound by Printing Express Ltd, Hong Kong

contents

Introduction

Hundreds of thousands of people are active birdwatchers, while millions of others feed the birds in their gardens, and specialist organizations, such as the RSPB (the Royal Society for the Protection of Birds) in the UK, have more than a million members. Birdwatching is a very popular pastime.

Why is birdwatching so fascinating?

Centuries ago, most birdwatchers were retired gentlemen or members of the clergy with an interest in the world around them. Decades ago, tens of thousands of people supported wild bird conservation, and many more fed the birds in their gardens, but only a few thousand went out to watch birds. So what is it about birds that grabs the attention of so many people nowadays? What is 'birdwatching' all about – what do these people do? This book tells you. There is nothing exclusive, nothing magic about it – except the birds themselves.

Watching birds can be a casual, simple matter, or it can become purposeful birdwatching, with an end in mind: or, for some people, encounters with wild birds can be intensely moving and stimulating. For most birdwatchers, there is something of all three – birds can be appreciated every day, as something that adds interest to the journey to work or the view from the kitchen window, but they can, at times, become the objects of a more serious, disciplined pursuit. And, now and then, there is an experience that transcends that and sticks in the memory as a magical moment.

This book will help you to start turning basic appreciation into something a little more determined – it doesn't have to be difficult, nor do you have to learn complicated subjects. Making your birdwatching more satisfying and giving it a purpose can start by observing the birds in your own garden. Knowing a little more about the subject generally gives any hobby more substance and generates greater satisfaction. That is the purpose of this book: to help you get more from birds and to enjoy them to the full.

▶ Kingfishers are surprisingly elusive for such colourful birds: a close encounter can be a memorable and magical experience for birdwatchers.

getting

started

Birds are the most visible and popular form of wildlife. They are everywhere you look; they are visible from your kitchen or office windows, from a car on the motorway or from a commuter train. Anyone who finds that birds can bring a bit of life and colour to their day can be a birdwatcher; there is nothing complicated about it.

What is a birdwatcher?

There is a difference between someone who simply enjoys having birds around, and a birdwatcher who wants to know more about these fascinating creatures. With the help of this book, you will learn how to make more of your interest and also how you can take it a step or two further. A passion for birdwatching can take you along many, varied roads.

Wonderful creatures

Birds are capable of feats that people cannot come close to without the most sophisticated technology. They survive out of doors in all weathers, from the equator nearly to the poles, from sea level almost to the height of Everest. Some can dive 100 metres or deeper in the ocean. They find their way around the globe without the aid of a map, a compass or a clock. Most of them fly well; many are masters of the air. No wonder we enjoy watching them.

Pursuing your interest

Birdwatching involves people in photography, drawing, painting and writing. However, you might prefer a more scientific approach, moving towards biology, ecology or conservation. Alternatively, you might want to become an expert in identifying birds, or you may take an interest in the rarities that you see. Many birdwatchers collect books or paintings, while others travel the world in search of birds, visiting wonderful places on the way. Who knows what you might choose to do?

With conservation in the forefront of public affairs and so many bodies now concerned with birds and their habitats, there may even be opportunities for employment in the bird world – the RSPB now employs as many as 1,500 staff during the peak times of the summer season.

MUST KNOW

Bird welfare
The welfare of the bird comes first. So long as what you do does not harm the birds, it is up to you what you do and how you do it. Some people are scathing in their criticism of rarity hunters (twitchers) and garden bird lovers (dudes) but who cares? There is enough to learn and enjoy about birds to suit everyone.

▶ Many of us begin with birds that are close to home, and nothing beats a robin, which is easily identifiable and comes to exhibit a special trust in humans who show their good intentions, especially by offering a mealworm or two.

What do I do?

Most people notice birds from their window or in some other everyday activity, such as walking to the bus stop, looking out of a train window on the way to work, or collecting the children from school. Sooner or later, there will be a song or a call that catches your attention, or a bird that always flies up to a particular perch, so you begin to wonder what it is, or why it is there. Take care – you might get hooked.

Identifying birds

The next step, once you have noticed that birds exist – surprisingly, perhaps, many people appear not to – is to find out what they are, or which is which. Bird books have the first bit of jargon to describe this: 'identification'. It sounds a bit daunting, maybe even a bit exclusive, and you might think that it's not for you after all.

However, don't worry about it – identification is just a term to describe how we can tell birds apart and distinguish them from each other. It will lead you into areas of knowledge and expertise that might surprise you. Knowing what a bird is can open up new opportunities for enjoyment – finding out more will increase your pleasure in your new interest, not lessen it.

MUST KNOW

Equipment
Apart from having no rules, birdwatching does not require vast amounts of kit. You can spend a fortune on the latest optical gear, cameras and digital equipment, but you can get along with almost nothing. However, you will need a pair of binoculars and a field guide.

◄ This pied wagtail can be recognized by its black, white and grey appearance and long tail, but its pale back and odd head pattern belong to winter and may be quite unlike the usual field guide illustration of a spring bird.

Birdwatchers' code of conduct

Birdwatchers should always follow the countryside code and apply their own code of conduct, too. The birds you are watching are always of prime concern. Getting a better view comes second to leaving the birds and their eggs, or chicks, undisturbed and free from unnecessary threats from predators.

- The welfare of the birds must come first.
- Habitats must be protected.
- Disturbance to birds and their habitats should be kept to a minimum.
- When you find a rare bird, think carefully about who you should tell.
- Do not harass rare migrants.
- Abide by the bird protection laws at all times.
- Respect the rights of landowners.
- Respect the rights of other people in the countryside.
- Make your records available to the local bird recorder.
- Behave abroad as you would when birdwatching at home.

Delving more deeply

You will soon find a level that suits you. If you stick at telling a wagtail from a thrush, a blackbird from a starling, a great tit from a chaffinch, that's fine. Plenty of people go little or no further yet they have a lifetime of enjoyment from the birds. However, it is more enjoyable to make progress and delve a bit more deeply into the lives of birds and the possibilities of birdwatching.

Sharing your enjoyment

You can learn by trial and error, which is often the most enjoyable way, if you have the time. But you may never know if you are getting it right or getting it wrong. Sooner or later you will want to find someone else who knows about birds, and there are several ways to do this. Behind the development of most identification experts there is usually a knowledgeable friend. Birdwatching can be a solitary pursuit, but it is best done with a friend who can share the excitements, give you some encouragement and also offer different opinions if you get stuck with an identification.

Binoculars

To do much more than watching from a window, you must have binoculars. They need not cost more than £50–100 but good ones may be £150–250, and some will set you back as much as a holiday in Spain. Get the best ones that you can reasonably afford, but don't worry if they are not incredibly expensive – many cheaper models will still give good results.

Choosing binoculars

Good binoculars will last a lifetime, so you should be comfortable with them. They should not be too heavy: a long day with heavy binoculars around your neck can be tiring. They should not be too big: you need to be able to handle them with ease, and use the focusing ring with a fingertip without changing your grip.

▲ Binoculars are essential for a birdwatcher: but they can be a once-in-a-lifetime purchase if you can afford to buy a good-quality pair. To make sure that they suit you, try them before you buy them.

Porroprisms and roofprisms

Most binoculars now come in two basic types:
- Porroprisms, which have a stepped shape (the traditional type).
- Roofprisms, which look straight-sided and are generally more compact.

Porroprisms give a better 3-D impression, because the larger lenses ('objective lenses') are further apart. People with large hands may find roofprisms a little small, whereas the larger, wider porroprisms are unwieldy for smaller hands.

Roofprisms tend to be lighter, and they have a more modern optical system (of lenses and prisms) inside. However, they are not necessarily better, and they are also more expensive.

Eyepieces

These come in several shapes and sizes, and you need to be sure they are comfortable and do not allow in too much light from the side. They may be deep (good if you like to press them

firmly against your eye sockets) or shallow (not so good if you like to push them hard against your eyes for better stability). Some models have retractable eye cups so that they fold flat or 'pop' down, thereby enabling you to use the binoculars while wearing spectacles, with only a minimal loss of field of view. Look carefully at these: rubber eye cups eventually wear out and may be expensive to replace, whereas 'pop up' types that snap into position may be dust-traps.

▲ Birdwatchers use a great variety of binoculars and telescopes and associated equipment, proving that there is no single correct answer to what is best: a lot depends on what size and weight suit you best.

▼ The traditional-shaped porroprisms have large lenses which are set further apart than the straighter-sided roofprisms (below left). They will give a better 3-D impression.

▲ Lightweight, compact and modern, roofprisms are handy to carry around.

Choosing the right specification

Decide on the magnification and the size of the objective lenses. These are shown by numbers that describe binoculars, such as 8x30 and 10x40. The first number is the magnification; the second is the width of the lens in millimetres.

Go for a magnification of 7, 8, 9 or 10. Six is a little too low; 12 or above is too high. Don't be tempted by binoculars that let you 'see craters on the moon' with a magnification of 20 or so. They will be too big, probably of inferior quality, and you simply won't be able to hold them still. Vibration, your heartbeat, and trembling hands all make the image dance in front of your eyes; the higher the magnification, the worse this will be.

Also, the higher the magnification, the more light is required (thus the wider the lenses) for a bright, clear image. So, while 8x30 is okay, 10x30 will be too dull: divide the first number into the second to get an idea of brightness. A pair of 7x50s will be really bright (7.1); 10x40 (4) will be less so but still better than 8x30 (3.7). Brightness is improved by the glass quality and the coatings applied to prisms and lenses, so very expensive 10x42s are likely to be beautiful to look through.

Why not go for 8x40 or similar? The smaller magnification is not a real handicap and it gives you closer focus, a brighter image and a wider field of view. They are likely to be cheaper than a pair of 10x binoculars of equal quality.

▲ Top-quality binoculars are expensive but brilliant, and can be a once-in-a-lifetime buy. You generally get what you pay for, but it is entirely your decision whether you think the top name makes are worth the extra cash.

MUST KNOW

Larger lenses

The problem with larger lenses is that they make the binoculars bigger and heavier, so you have to compromise: 10x50 sounds good but they are big; 10x40 might be a better bet. Also, the higher the magnification, the further away the binoculars will focus. It is fine to have 10x50s to look out over a reservoir or estuary but irritating if you use them in a wood and have to keep backing away to get a bird in focus.

Setting yourself up

Binoculars have two focusing wheels. One is the central focus that operates both sides together, and you will use this constantly. People will sometimes borrow binoculars and say, 'Don't worry, I won't change your setting', but they must see everything in a blur. You must change the setting; the focusing wheel adjusts to the distance to the object you are looking at and, since you are watching birds, they will be moving about all the time and therefore you must adjust your focus to match. You will need to change focus more with a higher magnification than a low one, which has a better depth of field.

The second focusing wheel, which is hidden away at one end or one side, is a wheel that adjusts the right-hand side. This wheel balances any difference between your eyes, so you set it, as accurately as you can, once and then leave it alone. Some products will have a click-stop or lockable eyepiece setting; others have a simple twisting eyepiece and this needs checking every so often, as it may rub against you and turn round after a time.

▼ Look at the grip on the binoculars that is being used here: one hand firmly grasps the body with the fingers ready to adjust the focusing wheel, while the other uses the fingertips (together with one elbow on a knee) to offer stability.

▲ It's a good idea to always have your binoculars slung around your neck on a comfortable strap just in case you see an interesting bird. If you keep them in their case, the bird may fly off before you get them out.

MUST KNOW

Useful tip
To help keep your binoculars steady, just stick one finger against your forehead, or a thumb against your chin.

Setting the eyepiece

To set your eyepiece, find something sharp and clear to look at, such as a pole or a road sign. Cover the right-hand lens, taking care not to get fingerprints on it, and focus the central wheel while looking only with your left eye. (It is best to keep your right eye open, to avoid strain and distortion.) Now cover the left lens, uncover the right, and look with your right eye. Don't touch the central wheel now. Just adjust the right-hand eyepiece: take it way out of focus first and then, with your eyes relaxed, bring it back until it is as sharp as you can get it.

This has balanced the two eyes, so you use only the central wheel from now on. Check the eyepiece setting every so often just to be sure; if you don't do this, you may have one eye always slightly blurred, which is not effective for seeing birds well and not good for your eyesight either.

Look after your binoculars

Don't go out with your binoculars in their case; hang them round your neck on the strap, so that they are 'at the ready'. Get a broader, slightly elastic strap if they are not comfortable, but keep them around your neck so you don't drop them or accidentally swing them against a wall or post. If you have them around your neck but have to jump a ditch, hold on to them: they are painful if they swing up and hit you in the teeth.

Clean the lenses occasionally – blow away any dust or grit before touching them and then wipe them gently with a soft cloth. Don't use water. Most of all, keep sticky fingers off the lenses. A rain guard is handy in wet weather and also to keep crumbs and drops of coffee off the lenses if you are having lunch out of doors.

In the car, the carrying case may be handy, but those little plastic lens caps are a waste of time. Make sure that your 'bins' aren't likely to fly off the seat if you stop suddenly. If you have left them out in the car overnight, warm them up before stepping outside on a cold day, otherwise you may have misted-up lenses for the first 10 minutes; that may be when the best bird flies by.

Using your binoculars

Using binoculars becomes easy with practice. The main thing is to 'get them on the bird' quickly: birds have a habit of flying off when you stop to look at them, so speed is vital.

● Don't look down at your binoculars, then raise your head and swing them around until you 'hit something', but bring them up to your eyes.

● Keep your head up and your eyes on the bird.

● Just raise the binoculars with your hands and put them directly to your eyes, so that you keep looking at the right spot.

● If you are waiting for a bird in a bush to pop up into view, focus the binoculars on the likely spot ready for action.

● Keep them raised to chin height so that you're prepared for it when the bird appears – but don't breathe into the lenses and mist them up.

▼ Fieldcraft involves getting close to the birds without disturbing them, and then manoeuvring into position to get a good view through your binoculars. Using them to their best advantage will come with practice.

Telescopes and tripods

A telescope magnifies things more than binoculars but you cannot 'see further'. With any optical equipment, you can only see exactly what can be viewed with the naked eye – it just gets bigger. On a foggy day, you will just see a bigger grey shape; against the light, you will see a bigger silhouette, so don't have unrealistic expectations.

Types of telescope

Telescopes are available in two main shapes: straight and angled.

● Straight means you look straight through at the bird and that you can point the telescope at it relatively easily.

● Angled means you look into the eyepiece, which is not aligned with the main body of the scope. This makes 'finding the bird' more difficult, but you can sit and look 'down' into the eyepiece more comfortably, or stand and do the same, without having to bend down and crick your neck. Thus tilting the scope upwards to watch something overhead is far easier, as you don't have to lie down on your back to do it.

Magnification

A telescope can enlarge a bird 20, 30 or 40 times. However, as with binoculars, the higher the magnification, the bigger the lens needs to be to get a bright image: 30x30 is hopeless, but 30x80, which is lovely and bright, is big, bulky and heavy. You will have to settle for a compromise in order to get the best quality at the best price, with the least weight and bulk.

MUST KNOW

Telescope tip
Always try to use the telescope with both eyes open: it helps reduce eyestrain, which can be a real problem if you use a telescope for long periods.

▶ Tripods, as used here for supporting a telescope, are solid and substantial and are ideal for cameras, too.

Tripods

The higher power makes the problems of a wobbly image much greater, too – somehow, you will need to hold a telescope very steady. A handy wall, fence or tree might help; otherwise you might have to sit down (maybe in a wet field) and balance the telescope on your knee (but modern 'scopes tend to be far too short for this to work). You will almost certainly prefer to use a tripod, and this means something even bigger, heavier and more ungainly to carry about with you all day long.

You can use a tripod with its legs closed up if you sit or kneel down; on a steep bank, you might have two legs closed up and one half extended to give stability and to ensure that the tripod is sitting comfortably on the bank. There are many ways to use a tripod; it does not have to be standing up with its legs fully extended.

▲ Tripods are more rigid and offer greater flexibility of use when just half extended, or with one leg extended to adjust for uneven ground, with the observer seated.

What to wear

There's a lot of nonsense talked about birdwatchers' clothing; people walk around popular reserves on a hot summer's day in camouflage gear and heavy boots, when jeans, a T-shirt and a pair of trainers would be more practical. However, it is up to you what you wear and you should aim to be comfortable, to be warm (or cool) and to be prepared for rain if it is forecast.

Clothing

Obviously, it makes sense not to be dressed in colours that are too bright, but a bird is likely to see you before you see it, even if you are in dull green. If your face and hands are pale, they are usually a giveaway at long range. So, don't worry too much about your clothing: in any case, most people make so much noise crunching on gravel, treading on sticks or chatting to each other that their camouflage clothing isn't going to be of much help.

There is such a wide range of superb outdoor clothing from which to choose, including good, breathable, waterproof but rustle-free fabrics which tend to do nicely, whatever the weather.

▼ The pale jacket stands out, but considering there are half a dozen people here, in an open wood, that may not be too much of a problem. The birds will have seen them anyway.

◀ It is important to be warm and comfortable when you are out birdwatching. A soft, lightweight modern jacket, woollen hat and boots are practical items of clothing.

Hats and footwear

Remember the special value of a warm hat on a cold day: most lost heat pours out of the top of your head so a hat will keep it in. Footwear is more difficult – you won't want to be in rubber boots all day. If you are going hill walking, be safe and wear strong walking boots: but for everyday birdwatching, everyday wear will usually do.

MUST KNOW

Umbrellas

If it rains, don't forget to take your umbrella out with you. People pay huge amounts of money for a waterproof jacket and still get wet, but a cheap umbrella tucked under one arm can keep you out birdwatching in steady rain without much problem. Few people do it, but I have enjoyed some excellent birdwatching from beneath an umbrella.

Using reference

One of the joys of many birdwatchers' lives is their bird book collection. Although you can spend a fortune on rare books, to most of us, books are there to be used and are bought for their practical value. You will need a good reference book right from the word go if you are to learn which bird is which, let alone find out more about them.

Field guides

A good 'field guide' is essential. Don't worry about the name – it doesn't mean that it isn't for you, even if you are only watching from a window. Birdwatching has its own language which tends to exclude a lot of people, but it should not. A field guide is simply a book that shows you how to tell the birds apart. Decide which one you like best and whether you prefer photographs or illustrations. Ideally, you should get one of each.

Photographs

Photographs are supposed to be 'real' but all kinds of problems are associated with them, such as heavy shadows, reflected colours (any 'white bird' is likely to have a range of greys, blues and browns within its 'white' plumage) and quirky shapes. Photographs 'freeze' birds in awkward positions, just like people – look at pictures of a football match and you will see what I mean.

Illustrations

Illustrations can remove these irrelevances and present the 'perfect bird' in a side-on pose, with its colours perfectly shown, but this depends on the skill of the artist and the quality of the printing. But artists have their own 'style', so their birds are not necessarily spot-on representations. It is probably best to buy a good illustrated guide with a photographic guide to supplement it.

▲ Field guides are a very useful identification tool for the birdwatcher. There are many to choose from, with either colour photographs or artwork illustrations.

Video and DVD guides

Videos are remarkably comprehensive and add real movement and 'character' to the static and sometimes unrepresentative photographs of books – the problem is finding what you want without having to spool backwards and forwards. DVD versions help solve this problem. They are brilliant supplements to the basic guidebook, but you still need a book to take out with you.

GARDEN BIRD SOUNDS

A sound guide to 70 garden birds of Britain

▲ Bird song CDs are a good way of learning to identify and distinguish between different bird vocalizations.

CDs

CDs of bird songs and calls are of wonderful quality. The arrival of the digital CD was a huge step forward in bird sound recordings, giving magnificently lifelike reproductions. They are also easier to use than tapes because you are able to find the right track instantly.

Ordnance Survey maps

At various scales, these maps can be a boon to birdwatchers. Some of us find maps beautiful, whereas others see them simply as practical tools. They can be invaluable in planning a birdwatching day or even a holiday. If you don't want to buy heaps of OS maps, you can still see them online if you have internet access: try the Ordnance Survey get-a-map website. Select the area you want to look at and zoom in to maps at various scales, planning your walks in advance.

MUST KNOW

Using the Internet
If you have access to the Internet, either at home or in your local library, you can learn a huge amount about birds. Try any search engine, such as Google, and just key in a species' name or the name of an organization, such as RSPB, BTO or BirdLife International. From these starting points, you can find many more links to other websites and you will soon learn your way around the most productive sites.

Keeping records

You may wish to keep some sort of record of what you see, and it is highly recommended that you do. Most of us like to know which birds we have seen, so you could easily become a 'lister'. However, recording what you have seen does not have to be obsessive or competitive – birdwatchers simply like to know what they have seen and what they have not.

▲ Keeping a bird diary is a good way of recording what you see. You might also like to make quick sketches out of doors of birds and their distinguishing features in a pocket notebook.

Keeping a bird diary

There are various ways of recording the birds you see, and a simple diary is an easy method, which has many advantages, especially if you keep it going for years. You need not record birds every day – just when you see something interesting. Use a simple ruled book, so that you're not constrained by a 'page a day' format; the entries can be as long or short as they need to be.

Making entries

Put the month in the top corner of each page, and start each entry with the day and date. Then list the birds in two, three or four columns (one takes up too much space) – keep them in some sort of order, even if only roughly (all the ducks, then the birds of prey, then the wading birds and so on). Add symbols if you like – stars for great views, underlinings for anything special, red capitals for a bird you've never seen before. You can add a bit of explanation at the bottom so you expand from a list to a more interesting and informative record of your birdwatching activities.

I've done this for years. The advantage is that you can look back to any date and see instantly where you were, what you did and what you saw. However, the disadvantage is that you cannot look up all your notes on any one species, or any single place, without having to trawl through years of diaries to find them all.

Other methods

The opposite way round, with the advantages and disadvantages reversed, is a card index system species by species, or perhaps based on places and sites. The best method, however, is to set up a computer system, so you can cross refer between all of these factors: you can find the record of a particular day but can also call up every occasion you have seen a firecrest or all the times you have been to a favourite lake or wood. It depends how much you like computers whether this becomes a joy or a chore.

Why keep notes?

Most people keep notes for their own amusement and information. We all learn from our observations and may even make useful contributions to ornithological knowledge. If we carefully note bird behaviour, for example, it adds greatly to the simple lists of species and numbers. But even species and numbers have value, as we shall see later in this book, and to use them, we must keep a record, somewhere. So a bird diary, card index or computer record becomes essential.

▼ How often do nuthatches visit your feeders? Do they come every day at the same times or in any particular season? Try to work out what might be influencing their visiting patterns and make a note in your records.

Photographing birds

Wildlife photography used to be highly specialized, expensive and difficult. A few famous pioneers, like Eric Hosking, made a living from it; some made films for television. Now, many people try, but relatively few make a go of it commercially. Nevertheless, the gap between the professional and the keen amateur has closed, through the introduction of top-class single lens reflex cameras, followed by the digital revolution.

Single lens reflex cameras

Pocket point-and-press cameras may have a zoom facility but the lens that takes the picture is separate from the viewfinder: you do not see exactly what you are taking. However, a single lens reflex camera uses a clever system of mirrors and prisms to make the light entering the main camera lens appear through the viewfinder. Only at the moment the shutter is released does all this optical gear flick out of the way to let light hit the film. You see exactly the picture you take. With interchangeable lenses, the photographer can also use long focus lenses to give extra magnification: to 'get in close' to the subject.

Conventional lenses with up to 300 or 400 mm focal length give decent magnification but are big and heavy: the mirror lens, a squat, wide piece of equipment, reduces the length, if not the weight.

◀ With a single lens reflex camera and modern colour films that work very fast (meaning shorter exposures are possible, even in quite dull light) and have smooth, rich colours, photographers can produce stunning results. But it still takes time, patience and skill, as well as a good knowledge of bird behaviour.

GETTING STARTED

Types of bird photography

There are two main kinds of bird photography: stalking, more or less out in the open, but using whatever cover you can find; and hide work, using an existing structure (such as a shed), a fixed hide at a nature reserve or a moveable or temporary hide that you build yourself.

▲ Photographing birds is an absorbing and rewarding pastime. There are many opportunities to exercise your hobby when you are at home watching garden birds, out for a walk in the countryside or on holiday.

Stalking

This is simply getting close to a bird by fieldcraft, i.e. creeping up through cover, even crawling along flat to the ground, until the bird is close enough to make a large image on the film. To do that, the bird has to be closer than you might think. Many people think they have a good picture, only to be seriously disappointed by the minute bird in the middle of a big picture when it is developed. A sub-category is 'wait and see' photography: perhaps sitting quietly beside a pond in a wood, waiting for birds to come to drink. Waiting at an open kitchen window for birds to visit the peanut basket is much the same, but gives a series of repetitive images after a while.

Hide work

Hides mean more work, more preparation, perhaps the use of private land where other people will not interfere. However, a hide will give more complete cover to the photographer, although sitting for hours in a minute 'tent' can be both tedious and backbreaking. The idea is to be close to the bird while it is unaware of the photographer's presence.

Hides were traditionally used near nests, but fortunately nest photography has largely gone out of fashion – it risks too much disturbance and, in any case, rare birds can only be approached at the nest with a proper licence.

But you can equally use a hide near a high-tide roost to get shots of waders and wildfowl, or beside a tip where gulls congregate, or by a gravel pit to get the best shots of passing coots, ducks, grebes and wagtails. A hide offers immense opportunities to get close to birds: a great privilege and a wonderful experience.

Wherever they are, hides must be used responsibly. If you get to the hide by a high tide roost an hour in advance of the birds, you may

▲ Fixed hides at nature reserves can be surprisingly good, but they have the disadvantage of being open to the public. You should take care not to 'take over' when other people wish to use the hide. Photographers should always be aware of other birdwatchers as well as the needs of the birds.

have to sit there for several hours until the tide recedes and the birds fly off. It would be wrong to get your pictures, then step out and scare the birds away after an hour. In every case, the bird photographer's motto is just like any birdwatcher's: the welfare of the bird always comes first.

Digital photography

This is no different from photography with film, except that you record images on a card instead of film. You can simply wipe off the images you don't want while you are out of doors and then download the ones that you do want on to a computer at home and use the card again. There is no expensive waste of film or development costs, once you are over the initial expense of buying the memory cards.

▲ A digital camera means that you can photograph the birds you see and view them on your computer at home. You can email the images to your birdwatcher friends and put them on a website.

You can easily e-mail pictures to friends or bird magazines, put them on a website or organize your own files, albums and slide shows. However, it is less easy to show your pictures to other people unless there is a computer to hand. Of course, you can print out the images as digital colour prints although the quality may not be so good as traditional processed prints.

Now everyone seems to be having a go. Public, permanent hides at nature reserves give close views of exciting birds. Digital cameras often have a good zoom lens: and expensive ones work just like single lens reflex cameras and have interchangeable telephoto lenses.

Digiscoping

For decades, astronomers have taken pictures through telescopes. Now birdwatchers are doing it: with an adapter, you can fasten your camera to a telescope and take a picture with it. The quality varies, but can be remarkably good. It is usually called 'digiscoping' but there is no reason why the camera has to be digital, really.

MUST KNOW

Be creative

Try to be imaginative, creative and artistic if you want to make a mark with your photos. There are plenty of side views of stock-still birds in perfect light perched on sticks: go for action, behaviour, something interesting. Try a bit of backlighting for atmosphere. Capture movement. As well as the standard super-perfect close up, there are increasing outlets for something different: maybe you can exploit them.

Making a start

Now that you're equipped and ready to start birdwatching in earnest, where do you go to see birds? You can head off to some woodland or open countryside, a reservoir or lake. However, your own garden may be the best place to start.

Where to watch birds

The best thing is to head for water which always offers so much more variety than dry land. You can also see the birds that live in habitats beside the water. Rivers are interesting and often lovely places to visit, but their birdlife is probably less varied than a good, lowland lake – lakes in the hills are often deep, cold, bleak and rather birdless. A good reservoir is often fine for birds, especially if it has natural edges, but even concrete ones have their moments. Most places

▼ Watery places mean that both water and land birds can be seen in the same area: almost guaranteeing you a greater variety of wildlife on a country walk.

are within reach of a flooded gravel pit. Such pits tend to have steep edges and no real mud (just gravel or sand) and are not so good as muddy reservoirs for wading birds, but they can be outstanding for ducks, grebes, gulls and even waterside birds such as herons and kingfishers.

Woodland seems the natural place to go to see birds, but it can be hard work in summer when the leaves are dense and dark, and also in winter when many birds move out of the woods into hedgerows and gardens. Woods are best for birds and at their most lovely in spring.

▲ Magpies provoke great differences of opinion: they are undoubtedly handsome, spectacular birds, but they eat eggs and young birds for a time in spring, which puts them on the 'hate' list of many people.

Feeding the birds

At home in the garden, new foods and feeders attract a wide variety of birds. Thus, such great birds as goldfinches and siskins are attracted by hanging feeders, while nestboxes help anything from spotted flycatchers and robins to tawny owls, swifts and starlings, as well as traditional nestbox birds, such as blue and great tits.

Feeding birds has become a multi-million pound industry in the UK. Look at the bird magazines for advertisements and get some catalogues and free bird-feeding guides – they give excellent advice, while, naturally, plugging their own products.

▶ Starlings are opportunists but are not ideally suited to feed on hard peanuts from a mesh feeder. They may rely on being able to take mashed pieces of peanuts broken up by other birds.

Bird tables

A bird table is not essential, but looks good and provides a fixed point for watching birds. A simple flat board on a post is best, or a board hung with a chain at each end (to stop tangling) from a branch. There is no need for a roof, but it may be helpful if you are plagued with pigeons and jackdaws and want to keep some food for the smaller birds – a low roof excludes bigger ones.

▼ Bird tables come into their own in bad winter weather, when small birds such as blue tits may find their natural food locked away under a layer of ice.

Hanging feeders

From trees, or from the edges of the bird table, hanging feeders are perfect, as they give birds space and food while allowing them to show off their acrobatic prowess. Feeders now come in two main types:

● The traditional mesh basket, made of non-rusting stainless steel.

● The plastic tube with 'ports' through which seed is dispensed at a controlled rate.

The basket type is useful for nuts, sunflower seeds and scraps, such as bits of fat and cheese that might even attract a great spotted woodpecker. The tube type is better for fine seed mixes. The finest, such as nyjer, may require a special feeder, as this tiny 'daisy seed' is easily blown away and wasted. It seems to work like magic in some gardens, bringing in goldfinches where none has been seen before within the hour, but for other people it's less successful.

◄ This is a tree sparrow, which can be identified by the brown cap and black cheek patch. However, it is now a rare bird on garden feeders across the UK.

Other feeders

You can also get all manner of seed hoppers, ground hoppers and caged-in feeders, which supposedly keep out squirrels and sparrowhawks. The ground hoppers help feed species of birds that prefer to be low down, but they keep food tidy, dry and fresh.

▲ Despite the protection offered by a mesh around the feeder, a sparrowhawk has managed to capture a small bird. It is an entirely natural occurrence and one we should expect from time to time if we attract small birds to our gardens.

◀ This feeder is intended to be squirrel-proof and it succeeds very well, but squirrels are famously difficult to deter for long.

Hygiene

It is essential to keep feeders and tables clean. From time to time, use a very mild solution of bleach (barely 10 per cent in water) and wash them down, then rinse thoroughly. Put food out as required: don't throw out tons of stuff and hope more birds will arrive – wasted food can rot, which is unsightly, potentially unhealthy and might attract rats. Adjust your supply to the demand.

Which foods?

Be inventive when you are feeding birds. You can smear some waste fat and cheese into the bark of old apple trees, for instance, to help treecreepers, tits and nuthatches. Remember that birds need high-fat diets; our low-fat fad is no use to them, as they need the energy. You can scatter currants and other unwanted fruit, crumbled pastry, crumbed bread and cake and so on around the edge of a flowerbed or hedge, to feed dunnocks and wrens, which would not usually come to a bird table.

Water

As well as all this food, water is essential for birds, even in winter. A bird bath is ideal, but you need to keep it clean and well topped up. It is best if it is shallow at the edges but deeper towards one end, so birds from blue tit to blackbird size can get in and bathe or drink. You may find that a flock of starlings descends on it and splashes all the water out within minutes, but they are great to watch, so welcome them in.

▲ A rough branch or a log can be loaded with nuts and fat in the crevices of its bark, thus giving it a more natural appearance to the birds in the garden.

▲ This blackbird is bathing in a shallow bird bath. Offering water in this way can be a lifeline to garden birds, all year round.

FOODS TO PROVIDE

- Bird seed mixtures containing flaked maize, sunflower seeds or peanut granules. Mixes containing chunks or whole nuts suitable only for winter feeding.
- Millet attracts house sparrows, dunnocks, finches, reed buntings and collared doves.
- Flaked maize is good for blackbirds.
- Black sunflower seeds are excellent year-round food.
- Nyjer seeds have a high oil content, need a special type of seed feeder and are good for goldfinches and siskins.
- Peanuts are rich in fat and popular with tits, greenfinches, house sparrows, nuthatches, great spotted woodpeckers and siskins. Do not offer peanuts in spring and summer unless they are in a fine mesh and cannot be removed whole.
- Cheese is a favourite with robins, dunnocks, blackbirds and song thrushes.
- Dried fruits, such as raisins, sultanas and currants, can be soaked and fed in spring and summer.
- Apples, pears and other fruit can be cut up.
- Pastry, cooked or uncooked, is excellent, especially if made with real fats.
- Cooked rice, brown or white, without added salt.
- Dry porridge oats or coarse oatmeal.
- Crumbled bread is suitable but in small quantities since its nutritional value is relatively low. Moisten if very dry. Brown bread is better than white.
- Fat, including suet, is welcomed by tits, great spotted woodpeckers, thrushes and wrens.
- Mealworms can be obtained from wild bird food suppliers.
- Waxworms are excellent but expensive.
- Fat balls and other fat-based food bars are excellent winter food. Make your own by pouring melted suet or lard onto a mixture of ingredients, e.g. seeds, nuts, dried fruit, oatmeal, cheese and cake.

WATCH OUT!

Foods to avoid

- Wheat and barley mixtures, which are suitable only for pigeons, doves and pheasants.
- Split peas, beans, dried rice or lentils, which attract only large species.
- Salted or dry-roasted peanuts.
- Polyunsaturated fats, low-fat spreads and other low-fat foods: birds need fat.
- Live foods and other insect foods.

Nestboxes

These are specialized garden equipment, but a simple tit box is easy to make. You can buy one but many of the models on sale are ridiculously small, with holes that are far too tiny. You need a hole of 28–35 mm according to species (a touch bigger for house sparrows) and a box, which is about 12 cm (5 in) square inside, with at least 15 cm (6 in) beneath the hole. Don't put a perch by the 'door', and make sure that you keep the box out of reach of cats if you can.

Woodpeckers can break into wooden boxes and eat the baby chicks inside, so a 'woodcrete' box (heavy, solid, concrete and sawdust mix) may be a good idea. Metal plates around the entrance hole are not very useful, as a woodpecker can go in at the side.

MUST KNOW

Nestboxes
For more details, you can contact the RSPB or look at a catalogue from a reputable bird food and garden bird equipment supplier – the birdwatching magazines have plenty of them.

▼ A baby blue tit calls from a nestbox; it is just about old enough to fly. Boxes can help birds where natural nest sites are absent.

A box with the top half of the front open, placed in a creeper on a wall or in a hedge, is good for robins and, if you are lucky, spotted flycatchers. You might try siting a row of three boxes under the eaves to help house sparrows – they like terraced accommodation. A bigger box with a larger hole could appeal to starlings.

Wildlife gardening

A good wildlife garden will be excellent for birds if it has plants that will attract insects (such as marjoram, thyme and St John's wort), produce berries (cotoneaster and pyracantha) or fruits (elder and ivy) or make plenty of seed (teasels and sunflowers). It all depends on your location and, especially, the size of your garden, but almost everyone can do something.

Gardening for wildlife really is worthwhile, and the results can be very satisfying. And there is always something very special indeed about building up trust with a wild bird and seeing it exceptionally close.

▲ There is scope to attract birds into small gardens.

want to know more?

Take it to the next level...

Go to...
▶ **Gardens and parks** – page 128
▶ **Urban fringes** – page 140
▶ **Woodland** – page 150

Other sources
▶ **Your local RSPB group or bird club**
   for local knowledge and expert tips
▶ **Your local library**
   for books on local birdlife
▶ **Internet**
   for information and personal experience
▶ **Gardening books and magazines**
   for plants that attract birds
▶ **Publications**
   visit www.collins.co.uk for Collins bird books

about

birds

All European birds can fly
(although some other birds,
elsewhere in the world, lost the
power of flight long ago) – but
so do bats and insects. All birds
lay eggs – but insects, reptiles,
fish and even a few mammals
also do this. So what makes
birds unique and different? As
we shall see, it is a combination
of features, plus a coating of
feathers, that sets birds apart
from all other creatures.

43

Bird anatomy

Birds are akin to reptiles; they are probably derived from small, active dinosaurs, although this is still the subject of controversy. They have bony skeletons with a backbone of many vertebrae (not unlike a reptile's), strong, slender ribs, a pelvis that supports the hind limbs, forelimbs with digits fused together towards the tips of the wings, a small, lightweight skull and bones that are light and penetrated by airways which allow great strength but reduce weight.

Designed for flight

A flying bird has a deep breastbone, or sternum, to which are attached strong pectoral muscles – the powerhouse for flight. A bird like a pheasant or woodpigeon has enormous muscles attached to the breastbone, giving a deep-chested shape and wonderful acceleration – high speed from a standing start which takes them away from predators. Other birds, such as kites and

▼ One of the biggest flying birds in the world today, the white-tailed eagle has broad, deeply fingered wingtips for powerful, stable flight.

vultures, have weak breast muscles but wings of very large surface area. They cannot beat them powerfully or quickly, but they ride air currents and glide superbly well – masters of the air, travelling far with almost no expenditure of effort. Between the two extremes there are many forms with greater or lesser power in the air.

Beaks, legs and feet

Birds have jaws which are clothed with tough, bony sheaths to give a strong beak; an upper mandible with little or no movement relative to the skull; and a lower mandible with considerable vertical, but little sideways, motion. Beaks are characteristic of birds but they vary greatly in both their shape and detail.

Birds' legs and feet may be fully feathered or quite bare, hard and scaly, with more or less arched 'nails' in the form of claws. Like beaks, legs and feet are strongly adapted to the way of life that is characteristic of a particular bird.

Parts of a bird

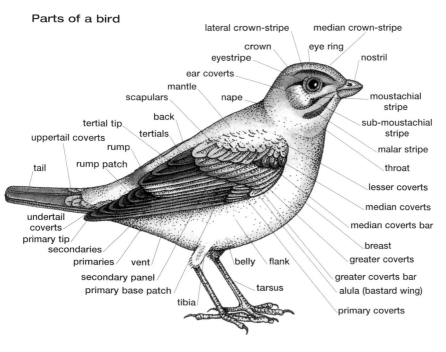

lateral crown-stripe
median crown-stripe
crown
eye ring
eyestripe
nostril
ear coverts
mantle
scapulars
nape
moustachial stripe
back
sub-moustachial stripe
tertial tip
tertials
uppertail coverts
malar stripe
rump
throat
tail
rump patch
lesser coverts
median coverts
median coverts bar
undertail coverts
breast
primary tip
greater coverts
secondaries
greater coverts bar
primaries
vent
belly
flank
alula (bastard wing)
secondary panel
tarsus
primary base patch
primary coverts
tibia

Feathers

A bird's feather is a remarkable structure. It is essentially composed of keratin, the horny substance that forms the basis for human fingernails. It is strong but light in weight, both of which are essential qualities for a bird.

The structure of feathers

Each feather has a more or less central shaft or, in the larger ones, a quill. Large quills have a hollow base and they taper to a solid, narrow tip. On each side is the 'vane' or 'web', composed of a complex structure of barbs, which grow out at an angle from the shaft, and barbules, which are like tiny hooks that zip together (a little like velcro attachments) and keep the barbs together as a strong, flat sheet. If the barbules become disarranged, a bird can simply 'zip' them together again by running the feather through its bill, otherwise known as preening.

Smaller feathers are loose with fewer interconnecting barbules. They form the soft down that insulates the bird beneath its covering of stronger 'contour' feathers, so called because they help shape the body into the characteristic form of each species.

Primary feathers
The wingtip feathers, called the primary feathers, are stiff and strong, but, in a fast, deep wingbeat, their tips will twist under pressure and act like miniature propellers, forcing the bird forwards as the wing is pushed down.

▼ Feathers add colour and pattern to a bird, as well as essential insulation and weatherproofing.

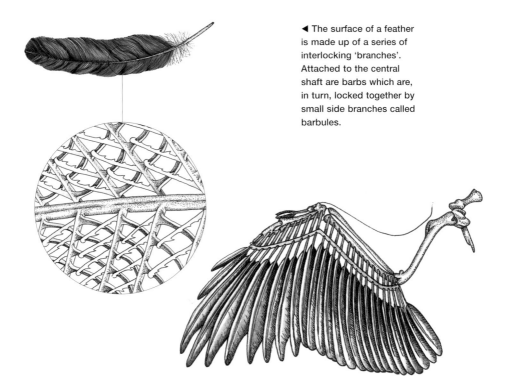

◄ The surface of a feather is made up of a series of interlocking 'branches'. Attached to the central shaft are barbs which are, in turn, locked together by small side branches called barbules.

The larger feathers on the wing and tail are the 'flight feathers'. They have a much stiffer shaft and strong vanes that are wider on one side than the other, to give an aerodynamic shape which helps the bird to fly.

▲ A bird's wing with all the smaller feathers removed. You can see that the bones are similar to those in a human arm.

Moulting and function

Feathers grow from 'germs' within the skin (the familiar 'goose pimples' on a plucked fowl) and can be shed and replaced once or twice each year, in a process called moult. In this way, they maintain a well-conditioned, sleek plumage that covers the body of a bird, growing from well-defined tracts over the skin.

Feathers provide warmth and insulation, waterproofing, colour and adornment, both in terms of pattern and shape. Without feathers, birds would have little or none of their uniquely colourful and dramatic character.

Flight

Birds are remarkable, not least for their ability to fly. They do not have the instant direction changes, acceleration and deceleration of insects, nor the ability to fly in total darkness shown by bats, but they are still truly expert.

The mechanics of flight

Flight is achieved by several means, often in combination. Pure power, from the large muscles in the breast, pulls the wings downwards and creates lift, by pressing the surface of the wings against the air. This, however, takes a huge amount of energy, and for larger birds, such powered flight may be short-lived. However, it can be extended by a glide – using the surface of the wing as an aerofoil to maintain height as the bird sails forwards through the air. For example, a pheasant, disturbed from the ground, rises with a great clatter of wings and flies off at great speed but, within seconds, has to glide on outstretched wings before landing at the run and dashing off into cover. It simply cannot maintain this high-speed escape for long.

▲ This gannet is about to land, with its legs dangling, tail slightly spread, head up and wings markedly angled – all designed to reduce speed and to add stability in the final approach.

Achieving lift

The upper surface of the bird's wing is convex, the lower surface flat or slightly concave, so air rushing over the top of the wing has further to travel than that beneath it. Air hitting the leading edge of the wing is split, half going above, half going below – to reach the back of the wing at the same time.

To avoid creating a vacuum, the air above must move faster. The pressure on the upper surface of the wing is reduced; the higher pressure below tends to push the bird upwards. This is exactly the same principle as that used in the design of an aircraft's wing.

Simple pressure against the air also pushes the bird higher, so long as it can move forwards and angle its wing slightly upwards. Forward motion can be gained by, for example, jumping from a cliff top, as a fulmar does when setting out to sea. But the bird might simply fly head-to-wind, using the movement of the wind currents to create lift against its wing surfaces.

Air currents

Seabirds use complex air currents very low over the waves, which take them hundreds of miles over the ocean with very little effort. Their long, narrow wings are perfect for such long-distance gliding, but they create so much force against the air beneath that they are not suited for quick wingbeats in powered flight.

▼ The long, narrow wings of this Arctic tern are made for long-distance flying and extra manoeuvrability when hovering and diving for fish. The tail streamers help it to 'steer' in its dive.

Soaring on thermals

Big soaring birds, such as storks, pelicans and vultures, seek out rising pockets of air, called thermals, which 'bubble' up over warm hillsides, and even roads and cities, and circle within them to gain a great height. Then they head to wherever they want to go and simply glide away, losing height very slowly to give forward motion and lift, as they simply use gravity to power their movements, with no effort at all. In soaring mode, they spread their long, broad wings to the utmost and their wingtip feathers are parted like 'fingers', to gain the greatest possible lift. In the downward glide, the wings are more angled with the feathers closed together to reduce drag.

▲ The broad, powerful wings of a white stork help it to gain height. When the bird is in a current of rising air, their great spread gives enormous lift and the stork can fly on with very little expenditure of energy.

Overcoming drag

Small birds, such as sparrows and finches, are so stout-bodied relative to their overall size that they have to overcome problems of drag: the friction of the air against their bodies, which slows them down. They do this by using fast bursts of deep wingbeats to thrust themselves forwards and upwards, then rest for a moment with their wings closed, diving forwards and downwards, until the next burst of beats. This gives them a characteristic swooping flight pattern.

Landing

When a bird comes in to land, it raises its head and body upwards and backwards, opens the alula as an airbrake, thrusts forward its feet, angles its wings and spreads its tail, using as much surface area as it can to slow down. By delicately adjusting its wings, tail and feet it makes a perfect touch down, whether on ground, water or a slender perch.

With small birds, such as blue tits landing on a nut basket, the action is so fast that we can hardly see it. To do this, a bird needs excellent eyesight and superb judgment; these must be instinctive, not calculated, in exactly the same way that we might reach up and catch a tennis ball. We could not 'calculate' the precise speed and angle of both the ball and hand but just 'catch it' without thinking. No doubt a bird flies and settles in just the same way, performing complex manoeuvres without having to think about what it is doing.

◄ One blue tit (lower right) is adjusting its position after settling, while another (centre) leans away and launches itself into the air before flying off.

Life cycle

Birds lay eggs and incubate them externally, in a nest, unlike mammals whose fertilized eggs grow internally inside a uterus. The nest is used solely to hold the eggs during incubation and, in many species, the chicks while they grow their first feathers. A nest is not a 'house' which is used all year round, although some nest holes and old nests may be used in winter as roost sites overnight, to keep a bird warm and sheltered.

Incubation

An egg has a yolk, a white and an air space, inside a fine membrane, within a calcium shell. It is 'incubated' – kept at a constant temperature while the embryo develops inside. The warmth is given to the egg from a bare patch of skin on the adult bird, called a 'brood patch', which is full of swollen blood vessels.

Most birds lay more than one egg over several days and incubate them together (as a 'clutch'). Some species, such as owls, incubate from the day the first egg is laid. As each egg hatches out after the same number of days, the chicks hatch out at intervals and the first-hatched are considerably larger than the last-hatched for several days, until all are fully grown.

MUST KNOW

When do birds lay their eggs?
Most birds lay their eggs in spring, from early April onwards, but a few, such as herons, mallards and collared doves, can lay eggs as early as February. How long they take to hatch will depend on their size – it can be as little as 10 days for the smallest birds, but up to 38 days for a mute swan.

◄ Here an Arctic skua is about to settle on its camouflaged eggs. It will turn them at intervals to prevent the membranes around the embryo becoming stuck to the inside of the eggshell.

Rearing the young

Many species, such as blackbirds and robins, lay several clutches during the course of a summer: they are multi-brooded. Blackbirds feed their young on earthworms, which are never super abundant, but they are usually available in small numbers for a longer period. Therefore they rear fewer young per brood, but three or four broods in the course of each year.

A single clutch

Other birds, as varied as swans, buzzards, owls and blue tits, lay only one clutch per year, literally putting all their eggs in one basket: they are single-brooded. In the case of large birds, such as swans and birds of prey, this is because the whole process of hatching eggs and rearing young takes so long that only one family can be reared per season. Blue and great tits, however, can rear a family in a few weeks but can only do so in spring; they need the short-term abundance of caterpillars in this season to feed their young.

Development of chicks

Once hatched, the chicks may be naked and blind at first and remain in the nest until they are well feathered and able to fly (as with songbirds and birds of prey) or they may leave the nest within hours, clothed in down and already able to walk, swim and feed themselves (as with ducklings and young wading birds).

Small birds, such as robins and wrens, are full grown when they leave the nest and independent within a week or 10 days, while big ones, such as swans and geese, may remain with their parents through their first winter of life, to be driven away next spring when they are almost a year old. This is a difficult time for most birds: many young kingfishers, for example, die when they are unable to find a vacant territory on a clean river.

▲ This great tit is feeding its chicks: the biggest and fittest get fed first, as it makes no sense wasting good food on sickly chicks that might die. If there is sufficient food, they will be fed later, and still survive.

Breeding systems

There are many different breeding systems used by birds. In some, such as that employed by the pheasant, the male mates with the female but takes no further part in incubating the eggs or looking after the chicks. The male may mate with several different females in a season. Other birds, such as the blackbird, share family duties and even split the family between them after they leave the nest, when they are able to fly but still dependent on their parents for food.

In many species, the female plays the greater part in incubation but the male takes the lion's share of finding food, both for the female as she tends the eggs and for the growing family afterwards. Some are bigamous, others are monogamous, but even in 'monogamous' species, such as the swallow, females take every opportunity to mate with other males. Many of their young are fathered by males other than their regular mates.

▼ Male pheasants fight fiercely to win the attentions of a female. It is the female bird, for all her duller colours, that has the final choice of mate.

A few species, such as the dotterel and red-necked phalarope, have reversed roles, in which the female lays eggs for the male to incubate, then leaves the area, so the male also has to look after the growing family. Others have more complicated roles, with a female laying eggs for her mate to hatch and another set for herself.

Young moorhens from the first brood of the spring help their parents feed young from later broods. Male long-tailed tits help their brothers rear families in complex social systems. Female dunnocks may have two mates, or males may have two females, in complicated triangles.

A few northern breeding birds, such as the sanderlings, have 'sequential polygamy', in which the female mates with one male and leaves him sitting on the eggs, then goes off to mate with another and lays a second clutch of eggs for him to incubate. These varied breeding strategies are fascinating and often surprising – even common garden birds are worth studying.

▲ A moorhen with its chick. Young moorhens reared in the spring may help their parents to feed small chicks from broods that are reared later in the summer.

MUST KNOW

Incubation

Most birds do not begin to incubate their eggs until the full clutch is laid, so that all hatch out more or less together and all the young are of the same size and age from the start. Young in the nest together are called a 'brood'.

What is a species?

A species is not a 'breed'. 'Breeds' are usually variations of an animal or plant which are produced by centuries of selective breeding; for instance, Cocker Spaniels, Chows and Greyhounds, and Scottish Blackfaces, Suffolks and Wensleydales, are breeds of dog and sheep respectively. The species are the dog and the sheep.

Bird species

Species arise naturally, but defining what they are exactly is not always easy. The concept that has been used over many years is that 'species are groups of interbreeding natural populations that are reproductively isolated from other such groups'. This works well when two different kinds of birds live in the same area. For example, blue and great tits are clearly distinct kinds because their breeding ranges overlap, but they don't mate with one another and are 'reproductively isolated'. They are kept separate by many things, including:

▲ The bold spots on this song thrush separate it from a blackbird. It is equally separate from the mistle thrush (below), although not always so easily identified.

- Their genetic make up
- Their appearance
- Their calls
- The details of their behaviour.

If they did interbreed ('crossbreed') to produce hybrid young, eventually the two kinds would merge into one.

◀ This mistle thrush shows the rounder spots, streaky wings and pale-tipped tail that separate it from the smaller song thrush. They are two distinct species, not merely 'varieties' of thrush.

◀ This hooded crow is different, visually, from the black carrion crow, but the colouring is superficial. Recent studies show that underlying differences are substantial, too.

Subject to interpretation

When similar birds live in separate areas, it can be difficult to decide whether they are different species. Western and eastern populations of the Bonelli's warbler were previously considered one species, but they have since been split into separate ones. When two populations live far apart we don't have any proof whether or not they would interbreed should they meet, so the decision as to what is a species becomes a matter of interpretation – a subjective judgement.

Hooded crows (with grey bodies) and carrion crows (all black) replace each other in different parts of Europe. In Ireland, the Isle of Man and most of northern Scotland, the crows are hooded; in the rest of Scotland, England and Wales, they are carrion. In Scotland, there is a narrow band where they hybridize.

The two have been considered 'subspecies' or 'races' of the 'crow' for decades, but recently they have been split and treated by scientists as two separate species. Something prevents 'hooded' crows becoming all black, and 'carrion' crows from becoming grey-bodied. There must be something beneficial about being one or the other that has maintained the difference in most cases over tens of thousands of years – good evidence that they really are separate species even though they mix a little, in a restricted area, where they meet.

▲ The carrion crow is all black, unlike the hooded crow which has a grey body and has been treated recently as a separate species – not just a race or subspecies – of the carrion crow.

▲ Arctic skuas are seen in several types. This one is a 'pale form' bird, but others are dark brown all over.

MUST KNOW

Polymorphic

There are polymorphic species with more than one variety, which can pair together and produce young of either type. The arctic skua comes in both dark and pale forms, but these behave alike. They can and do interbreed all the time.

A new definition?

There is a trend towards a new concept of species – the phylogenetic species concept – which says that different geographic forms of the same basic 'kind' of bird should be treated as distinct species. This is because these forms have evolved separately, and have unique evolutionary histories. There is no need to worry about whether they might interbreed. If they don't, they can be treated as full species. This would create many more species than we have been accustomed to.

Biological species concept

The traditional theory is the biological species concept, which is based on the idea that if genes can be shared between groups (because they can interbreed and produce healthy, fertile offspring), then these groups can and do influence each other genetically and are the same species.

However, the newer, phylogenetic species concept assumes that we can tell which groups are affecting each other genetically. If members of a group share a characteristic that is not found in other groups, such as white-fronted geese that breed in Greenland (dark plumaged, orange-billed) and Russia (paler and pink-billed), then they are separate, and they are clearly not spreading their features to the others. So they are separate species.

▼ The Greenland white-fronted goose is a tricky problem: is it a different race or is it a separate species altogether from the similar Russian-breeding white-fronted goose?

Varieties and variations

There are variations of birds that we can see, which are neither species nor subspecies. These differences are trivial and superficial, such as patches of white on a mildly abnormal blackbird, or the presence or absence of a white neck collar on a cock pheasant. This may be confusing initially.

How varieties arise

Varieties arise from centuries of domestication and selective breeding. Domestic ducks illustrate this well. They come from two kinds: the mallard (common in Europe) and the muscovy duck (a South American bird). Mallards gave rise to Aylesbury ducks (white with yellow beaks) and other types which can be all black-brown, brown with a white breast or a dull fawn colour, with a hint of a darker green head. Sometimes these 'farmyard' ducks go wild and mix with wild mallards. They are still the same species and can interbreed, but they don't interbreed with, for example, wild pintails or wigeon. You may see many variations as a result on a local lake.

▼ Mallards are true wild ducks but they are easily tamed and domesticated. Most farmyard varieties come from this species or from the South American muscovy duck.

ABOUT BIRDS

Unusual wild birds

Some genuinely wild birds look unusual. If they have too little pigment, which is a minor genetic fault, they may be extremely pale. For instance, you may have seen a sandy-brown sparrow or starling. These are 'leucistic' birds. With no pigment at all they become white (albinistic). With an excess of pigment (more rarely seen), they are very dark and are called 'melanistic'. There are really rare variations with too much red (erythristic) or yellow (xanthocroistic) but you are unlikely to see these.

Irregular patterns

You will often see individuals that are 'part albino' or 'part leucistic', such as crows with whitish wing bars (probably a result of poor nutrition), blackbirds with patches of white, and sparrows with white in the wings or tail. These patterns are irregular but often symmetrical. They may miss a generation but crop up again in later ones, rather like red hair or freckles in a human family.

▲ A blackbird with white patches is not infrequent; it is an individual variation, rather like someone with auburn hair – the variation is purely superficial.

MUST KNOW

Feathers

Some domestic bird variations have odd feathers: ducks with curly tufts on their heads and pigeons with strange plumes around their feet. These are obviously 'strange' and often too tame to confuse with some wild migrant out of its normal range.

Rarities

All of us like to see something unusual and unexpected. Rarities come in two kinds: some are birds that are simply very scarce, even in areas where they are regularly seen, while others are birds that have migrated too far north in spring – an 'overshoot' – or too far west in autumn.

Examples of rarities

Golden eagles are a good example of birds that are very scarce. They need huge ranges and they will never be abundant. Bitterns, on the other hand, need large areas of wet reedbed, a habitat so scarce that they are also rare and localized birds.

Birds that migrate off course might be storm-driven waifs, or may be so far off course that we can only assume that their internal navigation systems have somehow gone altogether wrong.

> **WATCH OUT!**
>
> **Be wary**
> Not all potential rarities turn out to be as exciting as you might hope. They are often escapees from zoos and ornamental wildfowl collections, e.g. flamingos or red-crested pochards. These are not genuine strays from far afield; they have strayed from an insecure aviary or park lake.

◄ Golden eagles are rare in England and are scarce in Scotland, but not 'rarities' as such in the UK. They are scarce local residents, rather than 'accidentals' which turn up outside their usual range.

Twitchers

Not so long ago, people had to find rarities for themselves – there was no 'grapevine' However, a network of people started to gather informally information from friends and contacts and give it to others, so a telephone network grew up that spread the news of rare birds more effectively.

Scores, then hundreds of people became interested in rare birds and, hearing of something interesting, would travel to see it at very short notice. These were the original twitchers. Twitching means travelling to see a particular, individual rare bird as a result of information received.

The media have misused the term and tend to apply it to birdwatchers in general. Nowadays, twitchers have pagers, mobile phones, e-mails and websites, all giving instant information about rarities and where they have turned up. Thousands of birdwatchers are on the move to see really rare birds, but few find their own. Much of the thrill is taken out of a rarity if it is just another on the list, found and identified by other people.

▲ Most birdwatchers are simply that – birdwatchers, or perhaps birders – but twitchers are different. They travel long distances to see a specific individual bird that they have heard of. Going out to see what you can see is not twitching, which has one particular bird as its target.

Migration

This is the regular, seasonal movement of whole populations of birds across the surface of the earth. Some birds stay in the same place all year but change their diet with the seasons, eating insects in summer and worms and berries in winter. Others eat insects all year but must move from place to place to find them – they migrate. Many birds migrate to exploit an abundance of food that is available only at certain times.

Heading north

The Arctic is fearsomely cold and dark from autumn to spring, but in the summer, it has twenty-four hours of daylight each day for a short period and, when the shallow soils and abundant pools thaw, insects and their larvae are superabundant and small mammals that hibernate all winter are active again. No birds can live there for many months, but during the summer months there is a fabulous food supply and huge numbers move north to exploit it. They include wading birds, wildfowl, gulls, terns and skuas, hooded crows and birds of prey.

▼ Migrating birds are often inconspicuous, travelling at night, but sometimes flocks of waders, starlings or geese show us that birds are on the move in numbers.

Wading birds

Wading birds heading to the Arctic in spring linger in their winter quarters until May – they have no need to go north until the snow and ice have melted. Then they rush north to find the best breeding territories, competing with fellow travellers as soon as they arrive.

Many are paired already, ready to nest as soon as they arrive on the tundra. To exploit the brief summer to the full they have strange breeding strategies: females often mate with several males and lay clutches of eggs for each to incubate. There is no time for a conventional pair to rear several broods in succession, as by early July they must start to head south. They can be seen in their 'winter' quarters for ten or eleven months of the year.

▲ A mixed flock of waders gathers on a shoreline as the tide comes in.

MUST KNOW

Arctic birds
Birds that breed across the whole of the Arctic from northern Canada to eastern Siberia flock to western Europe each autumn, where estuaries and marshes become vital refuges for several million.

Wildfowl

These also pair up in winter and dash north, ready to breed as soon as the conditions are right. That is why they are at their best, in full breeding colours, during the winter, and their summer colours are more subdued.

By late summer these birds have finished nesting and the adults move back south, at a more leisurely pace. Waders with a short, sharp northward migration in spring are now seen in much of Europe for several months in autumn: first the adults, later the young birds that move south without their parents.

Ducks, geese and swans behave differently, migrating as family parties, which can be seen together for most of the coming winter.

▼ A distinctive 'V' of geese at sunset is a beautiful and evocative sight in many areas near large lakes and coastal marshes.

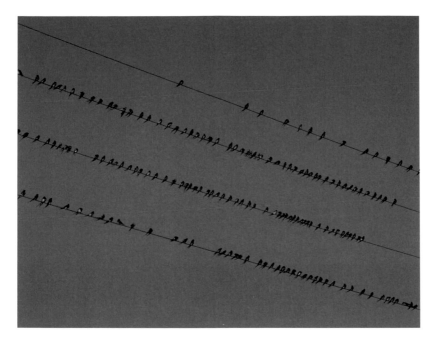

Heading south

Conditions are not so severe over much of
Europe, but most insect-eaters are still excluded
in winter and must go south to Africa to survive.
In spring, however, there is a rush northwards as
new food sources become available and many
millions of warblers, wagtails, pipits, swallows and
martins, small chats, flycatchers, finches and
others are on the move. The day length and
temperature control their movements.

▲ Swallows gather on wires
before migrating to Africa
in the autumn. They provide
us with a classic symbol of
the advancing seasons.

Summer visitors and migrants

In areas like the western coasts of Europe,
including the UK, and many Mediterranean
islands and headlands, resident birds are joined
by summer visitors and, for several months in
spring and autumn, 'passage' migrants, too, on
their way north or south. These periods are
exciting for the birdwatcher as there is so much
to see, so many birds migrating: each day may
bring new arrivals and unexpected finds.

Swallows

Swallows trickle north in small parties in early spring, but gather in flocks to move back south in autumn, roosting together in tens of thousands in reedbeds on the way. Some five million swallows leave Britain and Ireland every autumn. They cross the narrowest part of the English Channel before moving south into Africa.

The toughest part of the journey is crossing the Sahara to Nigeria and Ghana, the only time when they need extra fat as fuel – the rest of the time, they feed as they go. They reach Africa after eight to ten weeks but in spring return more determinedly, in six or seven weeks, wanting to get back to claim the best possible breeding territories.

▲ These swallows have settled in a bed of reeds, in which flocks sometimes spend the night, safe from predators, during their migratory journeys.

MUST KNOW

Adverse conditions

Most migration takes place at night, when birds can see the stars in a clear sky. We may view few birds on the ground in such conditions. When we see large numbers of wheatears, flycatchers, warblers and goldcrests on the coast, it is a sign that the weather caught them out overnight and they were forced down by fog, rain or strong winds. To us, this is a 'fall' of migrants; for the birds, it means difficult conditions.

Swifts

These birds feed solely on aerial insects and reach northern Europe as late as May or early June; they head south again by August. They breed in Europe but spend most of their lives in Africa. The young swift does not settle again after leaving the nest for twenty-three months, a first flight of some 350,000 miles. Our swifts ride the winds over West Africa for the autumn, then drift south-east to spend the winter in East Africa.

Small birds

These may migrate from 2,500 to 7,000 miles, putting on weight under the control of special hormones. Warblers have several migration strategies. Short-winged chiffchaffs move to southern Europe; a few even stay in Britain for the winter. Longer-winged but otherwise similar willow warblers travel to East Africa for the winter. Whitethroats cross the Sahara, while lesser whitethroats travel south-east in autumn to go to south-west Asia beyond the eastern Mediterranean. Sedge warblers double their weight with fat in autumn, to take them on a huge flight south to Africa in one go. Garden warblers, normally weighing around 15–16 g, eat berries as fast as they can in late summer and autumn, and leave at a weight of 40 g, loaded with fuel for the great migratory journey ahead.

Different strategies

Some similar pairs of birds have different strategies. The stonechat has larger broods of young than the similar whinchat, but remains in the UK in winter, where it risks death in spells of very severe cold weather. Survivors can, however, with their large broods, recover quickly from such disasters. Whinchats leave Europe for Africa, risking death on their long journeys; they rear fewer chicks but avoid the cold. The two strategies more or less balance out.

◄ A garden warbler will double its weight by putting on layers of fat during the autumn. These provide fuel for its mammoth migration flights that may keep it aloft for two days or more.

ABOUT BIRDS

Traditional routes

While a young Bewick's swan or barnacle goose will follow its parents on their long journeys and learn traditional routes and stopping places that have been used for tens of thousands of years, the young sanderling, or cuckoo, will fly south alone, with no such assistance, no clues from birds that have done it before. Yet waders, such as sanderlings and knots, and other birds, like Arctic terns, will fly from the northernmost land in the Arctic to the southern tips of South America, Africa and Australasia in epic annual journeys.

Returning to the same place

Swallows that nest in the shed next door will return to the very same shed the following year. Willow warblers will sing from the very same tree as the previous spring, and, remarkably, also from the same bush on the African savannah during each winter. Ospreys that nest in treetop eyries in Scotland return to the same nest each spring after spending the winter in West Africa. Young gannets that have been reared on a Scottish island move south to the rich fishing off Africa where they spend a year or two of immaturity before moving north again, but they will almost certainly return to their native colony. The homing abilities of a great variety of birds are truly remarkable.

Numbered rings

Most of what we know about such amazing feats has been discovered through decades of marking live birds with numbered rings. The birds are released unharmed; if they are later caught again, or found dead, the details on the ring can help us to trace their movements. If you find a ring, return it to the address stamped upon it.

◄ Kittiwakes make a fine sight on their nesting ledges.

How do they do it?

We know many of the mechanisms that birds use, but migration remains a magical process. Birds must have an accurate internal clock and calendar. Young birds learn the star patterns overhead and the position of the sun, but these are of no use unless they can be related to the time of day, the season and the position on the earth's surface from which they are observed. Land birds learn the contours of the landscapes around them, probably in remarkable detail, so they can home in on their nesting areas once they are in the general vicinity, but seabirds, flying a metre or two above the waves, have no such visible clues.

Some birds have special secretions in their brains, even inside their eyes, that detect the earth's magnetic field – the robin's right eye is used in this way. They see polarized light and thus can use the position of the sun even on cloudy days. In several ways, they are able to orientate themselves and pinpoint their position on the earth's surface.

▲ Ospreys will return to the same nest each spring.

want to know more?

Take it to the next level...

Go to...
▶ **Identifying birds** – page 72
▶ **Habitats for birds** – page 116
▶ **Your local patch** – page 184

Other sources
▶ **Catalogues**
  for buying bird foods and feeders
▶ **Videos and DVDs**
  for more information on birds
▶ **Field guides**
  for identifying unfamiliar species
▶ **Internet**
  for information on migration
▶ **Publications**
  visit www.collins.co.uk for Collins bird books

identifying

birds

Identification will come with practice. Some birds are easy to see and relatively simple to identify, whereas others are unique in their appearance but much harder to spot. However, many birds look more or less like other species and it may be difficult to get a positive identification. You will need to study them carefully and get good views to be sure of what they are.

Telling birds apart

Like anything else, bird identification becomes easier with
practice, and it takes time to become an expert. No-one
expects to learn how to play a piano or become a top-class
footballer over a weekend, but many people seem to think
that identifying birds can be learned while on holiday or over
a few weekends. To be really expert may take years, but
these will be years of great pleasure.

The basics of identification

We are all always in the process of learning and
developing our hobby. You will soon progress far
beyond 'identifying' the commoner birds – you will
just 'recognize' them (as you already will with
magpies) as you do members of your family, or
your favourite type of car; you don't need to
check a series of 'field marks' every time.

    However, even garden birds may be difficult to
identify at first: they tend to fly away against the
sky, or sit like tiny dark spots at the top of a tree,
or disappear into the foliage of a shrubbery and
not come out. Don't worry if this happens to you;
identification will seem difficult and confusing at
first but it rapidly becomes easier.

▼ 'Blackbird' sounds easy,
but not all these birds are
black: females are dark
brown; and juveniles (below)
are rufous-brown with paler
spots above and dark spots
beneath. They are never as
pale and clearly spotted as
a song thrush, but the
spotting reveals that the
blackbird is a true thrush,
nevertheless.

▲ The marsh tit (above) and the willow tit (left) are remarkably hard to tell apart. Using their different calls is the best way, but there are subtle differences in plumage and shape. Notice the willow tit's thicker neck and proportionately larger head.

A good field guide (see page 24) is helpful, but a knowledgeable friend is a bonus. It is possible to sit and work things out for yourself, however, and this is really the best and most satisfying way, so long as you have the time.

Don't jump to conclusions

Check out all the possibilities before deciding. It is easy to flick through a book until you come to a picture that looks something like the bird you have seen and think it must have been that, but this is often unlikely, especially if the bird you saw was in a garden in Hampshire and the one in the book is only found in the mountains of eastern Europe. There are many clues buried away in a good field guide.

MUST KNOW

Basic checklist

If you think you have found the bird you have seen in a book, check out the following points:

- Is it found in the area where you saw it?
- Does it live in that habitat?
- Is it there at that time of year?

These are basic things to check. Many birds are found in Europe only in spring, summer and early autumn; many others only in autumn, winter and early spring. If a bird is usually found in a forest, you are unlikely to see it on an open field. If it is a bird of freshwater marshes, the chances are that it will not be in your garden.

All of us start off by trying to match what we have seen with the pictures in a book, but look at the maps, the habitat details and the time of year when it is in your area (if it visits at all). Then try to consider other possibilities, such as closely similar species that have to be ruled out.

▼ Few birds look like the lapwing: but with others, you may have to narrow down the possibilities from several similar species.

Species and families

You will notice that many birds can be grouped into similar species: these are usually obvious families, such as warblers, thrushes, birds of prey and ducks. Learn more about these families and why and how they differ from others, especially what makes the birds of one family similar to each other but not like the rest? For example, ducks swim and have webbed feet, but birds of prey have sharp claws and hooked beaks.

Other differences are more subtle: tits are small, chunky, active, short-billed, stubby-footed birds that bounce and jump about in foliage and dart from tree to tree. Warblers are also small, but are sleeker, less squat, often with longer, slimmer tails, longer, thinner bills, and more sedate, relaxed actions as they slip through foliage in trees, bushes or waterside plants. Pipits, however, are also slim and thin-billed, but they have longer legs, bigger feet, longer tails with white sides, and walk about on the ground.

▲ Skylarks have small crests, rather stout beaks and strong legs; they are essentially streaky brown.

▲ Meadow pipits are streaky brown, but show thinner bills and legs than larks. This one is ruffled up against the cold, belying its slimmer build.

▲ There are two kinds of godwit in Europe. This is the bar-tailed, with relatively short legs but a very long, slightly upcurved bill.

MUST KNOW

Elimination

The information in this book will help you to get things sorted out and, by elimination, you will get new birds down to one or two possible families, then into smaller groups, perhaps into just two or three possibilities. When you go into details, such as the size and shape, you should be able to pin down what you are seeing.

Scientific names

Families are not always obvious from their English names: thus, a blackbird is a thrush, a linnet is a finch and a blackcap is a warbler. What will help you understand more about their relationships are the birds' scientific names: two-word names in italic print often written after the English name.

The first word shows the bird's genus: so the mallard, teal, gadwall and shoveler, for example, are all ducks in the genus *Anas*, while the falcons are *Falco*, harriers *Circus* and hawks *Accipiter*. You don't need to learn these and no-one usually uses them in conversation (unlike botanists) but you will find it useful to notice them in your guide books.

They help you to split larger groups into smaller ones. For instance, warblers come in various types, including *Phylloscopus* (small, greenish, sleek birds with sweet 'hoeet' calls, of bushes and trees), *Acrocephalus* (small, brown, streaked or plain ones, with guttural calls, of waterside reeds and sedges) and *Sylvia* (a variable group, often more colourful, with male and female different, short, hard calls but musical songs, found in shrubs, trees and low scrub).

Size

What size is the bird, roughly? It is hard to compare a bird with something familiar, such as a drink can, an apple, or a size 10 shoe, because things are never quite the same shape. An impression of 'size' is usually more to do with bulk, which is better expressed by weight than the length from beak to tail (what the books tell you). If you can, compare a strange bird with something nearby, or judge it against your mental impressions of common ones: say, a blue tit, house sparrow, blackbird, pigeon, mallard or goose.

Shape

What about the bird's shape? Try to compare it with something you know: is it pigeon-like, or like a dove except that it had much longer legs, or roughly like a chaffinch but with a thinner bill?

If you can, note down the details, especially bill shape, leg length and the shape and length of the tail. Some birds have very distinctive shapes, such as the long neck of a swan, the lyre-shaped tail of a black grouse or the round body and long tail of a long-tailed tit, but many others are not especially distinctive. It might be a thick, thin, straight or curved bill that gives a crucial clue.

▲ Black grouse are striking birds when they are out in the open, looking like big, black cockerels.

▼ The curlew is our largest so-called 'wader', but other kinds of bird also wade, including the much bigger grey heron.

Colours and patterns

When you are out birdwatching and you see an unfamiliar bird, you should try to get a good idea of its basic colour and pattern. Always jot down some notes or do a quick sketch in your notebook to describe what you see.

Distinctive markings

If you spot a bird that you cannot identify, you must ask yourself some basic questions. What is the basic body colour? Is it different above and below or is it roughly the same? Is it dark or pale?

As quickly as you can, get an idea of a pattern that stands out. What catches your eye? Does the bird have a stripe over or through its eyes? Stripes over the eye (superciliary or eyebrow stripes) are usually pale; stripes through the eye (eyestripes) are often dark. Are there marks on the wings: when closed or open in flight? Birds such as chaffinches have pale wingbars; some ducks and many wading birds have long pale stripes along the open wing.

Look at the tail: especially in flight when it may show patches of colour at the base or on either side, or stripes of white along each edge. Once you know more about groups of birds, you will remember what to look at most closely for identification purposes.

▲ Look at the pale feather edgings on the wings of this chaffinch, as well as its greenish rump, chestnut back and greyer head.

MUST KNOW

Scientific names

Good identification guides will feature birds' Latin names; these are always in italics and consist of two words. The first word helps show which birds are closely related, such as the chaffinch and brambling (both *Fringilla*) or the linnet and twite (both *Carduelis*). This is helpful in identification: the *Fringilla* pair are much more like each other than any *Carduelis* finch in shape, pattern, flight action, behaviour and call notes.

Wading birds

Redshanks, godwits and sandpipers have bill and leg colours in different combinations, and patterns on their wings and rumps. But if you think you are looking at a curlew or a whimbrel, the leg and wing colours will not help you: you must look at the head and listen to their calls.

Warblers

With warblers, eyestripes and leg colours may be the best clues; finches have different coloured stripes and bars on their wings.

Tits

Tits visiting the bird table may have bright yellow on them (blue and great tits) or no yellow; blue and green or just brown. Blue and great tits are told apart by the patterns on their heads; the brown ones by wingbars (or not), a white patch on the back of the head (or not) and more subtle differences, including their calls.

Persevere

If all this sounds too daunting, don't be put off. Remember, you can't get familiar with birds in a single weekend; it may take years, and you will still be learning after a lifetime. However, you will enjoy every minute of it.

◀ A black-headed gull in summer (top) has a very dark brown hood. In winter (bottom) the head feathers are moulted and replaced with white ones, except for the dark cheek spot.

Changing feathers

The colours of feathers are created by pigments or, in some cases, such as the electric blue of the kingfisher, by reflections of light (like those on a CD or from oil on water). Once a feather has grown, its basic colour and pattern are fixed, but it can still change in various ways.

▲ The pale stripe over the eye and barred wings show that this is a wren, apart from its characteristically upright tail and round shape.

Patterns and colours

These may vary within a species according to age, season and sex. Some, such as the wren and carrion crow, have little or no variation and look the same at any time. Others, such as large gulls, may take several years to become fully adult and will have a series of intermediate plumages, as well as summer and winter variations for each. Most small birds, however, have a recognizable juvenile plumage which soon changes into the adult pattern. Some, such as the song thrush, have the same colours whether they are male or female, whereas male and female blackbirds, for example, are very different.

Constant colours

It is astonishing how remarkably alike most individuals of any one species, age and sex are. For example, the pink on a male bullfinch in England is almost identical to that of every other male bullfinch in England: so much so, in fact, that the slightly deeper pink of a bullfinch from Scandinavia is immediately obvious should one stray across to the UK.

Every UK robin looks like every other UK robin, although visiting robins from the continent are perceptibly paler. Millions of black-headed gulls have precisely the same shade of grey on their wings and backs. The bottle green on a mallard's head is just the same on the heads of millions of mallards.

Constant patterns

Their patterns, too, are surprisingly alike, right
down to the finest detail. Rare birds, such as the
very similar Blyth's and Richard's pipits, can be
told apart by the shape of the dark centres on a
handful of their wing feathers.

More basic patterns are usually relatively
constant: for example, while adult sparrowhawks
and goshawks are barred crosswise underneath,
young sparrowhawks are barred while young
goshawks are striped lengthwise. Reed buntings
always have white sides to their tails, but corn
buntings never do. Woodpigeons always have a
white band on each wing; stock doves never do.

Such constant patterns are vitally important
as an aid to identification; otherwise we would
never succeed. They allow us to find 'diagnostic'
differences. If we see a grey or golden plover,
and it raises a wing to show a black 'armpit'
patch, we will know with 100 per cent certainty
that it is a grey. A ringed plover has a white
wingbar; a little ringed plover never has one.

▼ Kingfishers change their
colour according to the
light, looking more green,
or more blue, because their
colours come from the
reflections from the feathers
rather than from proper
pigmentation.

MUST KNOW

Wingtip feathers

There are other details that are remarkably constant. People who catch birds to ring them and then release them can identify similar species by the relative lengths of their wingtip feathers – this phenomenon is known as the wing formula. In the same way that we have our middle finger longer than the others, many birds have distinctive wing formulae, so, for example, the chiffchaff (with its rather short, round wing) can be distinguished from the willow warbler (with its longer, more pointed wing) when the relative lengths of their wingtip feathers are compared.

Moulting

Birds do change colour, and even their shape, from season to season, and as they grow from juveniles just out of the nest to being fully adult, so how do they do it? Feathers are shed, usually once or twice a year, and replaced by new ones in a process called moult. However, they don't simply fall like autumn leaves in any old order: the process and its timing is remarkably precise.

▼ Here we see herring and lesser black-backed gulls in their various plumages. They vary greatly according to age and season, but not sex, and thus present us with some interesting identification challenges.

Gulls

Take, as an example, a gull (which is big, so you can see moult in action quite easily). The young chick grows feathers in a few weeks after hatching, and it makes its first flight in this first covering of feathers, which is called 'juvenile' plumage. Very soon, it replaces the feathers of its head and body, but the bigger, stronger ones of the wings and tail remain. This, the 'first winter' plumage, lasts through to spring. Then it replaces the feathers of its head and body once again to acquire the 'first summer plumage', and begins to look more like an adult.

In the late summer and autumn, it then replaces all of its feathers for the first time: the wing and tail feathers are now a year old. The first feather to drop is the innermost 'primary', one of the big feathers just behind the bend of the wing. As the complete moult continues, so one primary after another is shed, so that, when the whole moult is complete, the very outermost wingtip feather is the last to grow. Because of this phenomenon, we are able to measure the progress of most birds' moult by the state of their primary feathers.

▲ Gulls, such as these black-headed gulls, are large enough to show their feather patterns well at moderate range, so you can easily recognize when they are moulting, or where there are mixed ages in one flock, as there are here.

▲ This great black-backed gull chick is still in down: it is best identified by the parent that comes to feed it.

Other plumage changes

There is another way whereby colour and pattern can change. Take the male chaffinch: in winter, its head is mottled with sandy-brown and grey. Each feather is actually blue-grey with a broad sandy tip. By late winter, the sandy tip crumbles away, as if at some internal signal, and the blue-grey is revealed. So a winter chaffinch has a dull, brownish head, but a spring one has a clean blue-grey head, without actually moulting any feathers at all. At the same time, the bill changes from yellowish to silvery-blue to complete the makeover.

Abrasion and bleaching

Colours can change in another way without a single feather being shed. This is through wear (or abrasion) or bleaching. Dark brown hair may become streaked with blond in sunny summers; in the same way, a dark feather becomes paler after several months of exposure to sunlight. It is instructive to pick up feathers from a lawn or beach. Often you may see the tip and outer edge are paler than the base and inner edge: the dark area is where the adjacent feather has covered it and kept the original colour fresh and dark; the paler part shows the effects of the sun.

▲ The male chaffinch is dull in winter, with its brown feather tips obscuring the brighter, paler, bluer colours on the bird's head that appear in spring.

MUST KNOW

Robins

Wear and tear and bleaching in the sun affect the colour of birds. An autumn robin will be richly coloured and the red will still be intense in the spring. By late summer, its plumage is battered, pale and dull. It hides away while it moults, reappearing in late autumn, fresh and bright again in a new set of feathers.

The black wingtips of gulls turn browner with age and the effects of sun and salt. The blue, green and purple sheen of a magpie becomes dull as the feathers get old and lose their perfect reflections. Old feathers have slightly ragged, untidy edges: they may even be worn down to the shaft at the tip.

Pale parts of feathers are most susceptible to wear. The dark pigment is usually melanin, which not only colours a feather but also strengthens it. Going back to our gull wingtips, feathers that are black with white spots tend to lose the white parts by the end of the summer, as the white is weaker and wears away much more quickly than the black. Birds such as the curlew, golden plover and skylark have dark brown feathers with pale spots, in a dog-tooth shape, along their edges in winter. By late spring, they look more uniform and dull, as the pale spots wear off, leaving all-dark feathers with saw-tooth edges.

▼ This bird is a curlew sandpiper in autumn. It is moulting from its red summer plumage to the grey and white of winter. The patterned feathers on its back are summer ones, and are being replaced by new, plainer grey ones, which are easy to see.

Why different colours?

Birds can change their appearance according to their age, sex and the season. They have evolved different colours and patterns for many reasons, the main ones, as we shall discover, being advertisement and camouflage.

Different requirements

Different birds have totally different requirements when it comes to colour. For instance, a mute swan is huge: it has few obvious enemies and little need to hide. Instead, it needs to advertise the fact that it exists to other swans, over long distances. It needs to attract a mate but it also has to have a territory in which it can nest, feed and rear its young, free from competing swans. The best colour to catch the eye of other swans is plain, bright white.

However, a female mallard is a good meal for a fox. She must sit on the nest to incubate her eggs for weeks: the important thing is to be inconspicuous. The best colour for hiding away in long grass and under bushes is a streaky brown. The mallard's plumage is perfect for concealment. These two extremes illustrate two entirely different requirements: advertisement and camouflage.

▼ A mute swan is so big that camouflage is of little use to it. It is stark white, a simple statement of its presence to other swans for miles around.

IDENTIFYING BIRDS

Camouflage patterning

Camouflage works for predators as well as prey. Sparrowhawks can be inconspicuous when they are hiding in trees waiting for an unwary bird to come close. Camouflage patterning is called 'cryptic plumage'.

Such patterns start with the egg, and thus a ringed plover's egg is mottled, to break up its outline which is otherwise given away by light and shade on the smooth, curved surface. It is coloured exactly like the shingly beach on which it is laid. The downy chick also has bold patterns that make it difficult for us – or a predator – to spot the 'round, fluffy chick'. The lines and spots interfere with the shape of the chick when it stays stock-still against a background of sand, stones and shells, helping it to merge into the shapeless patterns around it.

The black and white bands on an adult ringed plover do the same: at a glance, we can see a shapeless, incoherent patch of dark and light marks instead of the head and body of a bird. A black line through the eye is a common pattern on a bird, removing the tell-tale round, dark eye that will otherwise be easier to see.

▲ A lapwing chick will sit still when its parent calls; it is almost impossible to see for as long as it does not move. Any movement might give it away to a predator.

MUST KNOW

Camouflage

Artists developed camouflage for warships at sea: they were not painted dull green or blue, but a strong 'dazzle' pattern to break up the ship's outline. Birds use the same technique: their patterns look strong and obvious close up, but become hard to see at a distance when their shape is disrupted.

Examples of camouflage

Some good examples of camouflage include birds as different as:

● Woodcocks: a 'dead leaf' pattern, ideal for the woodland floor.

● Nightjars: perfect for hiding against a log or heathy ground

● Ptarmigans: look exactly like a lichen-covered rock. They even change with the seasons, being white in winter, mottled in spring, and salt-and-pepper grey in summer to adjust to their changing mountain top environment.

▲ Few birds are so beautifully matched to their background as the woodcock on a woodland floor.

Countershading

Many birds are paler underneath than they are on top. This is called 'countershading'. It is a simple way to reduce the effect of light (from above) and shade (below), which would otherwise highlight the shape of a bird against a flat background. Instead, we see the dark area lit from above, and the pale area in shade below, creating a flatter, more uniform effect.

Some birds, such as stone-curlews on short, dry grass, effectively 'disappear' against their typical habitats. Even the upper edge of the flank on a song thrush or robin, for example, which often catches the light, is a fraction darker than the rest of the underparts to minimize the effect of sunlight from above.

▲ Female swallows prefer male birds which have long tails and sleek, richly coloured plumage.

Advertising colours

'Right is might' in most cases when male birds threaten each other. The male on his territory usually succeeds in driving away an intruder, but should he then cross the boundary, the positions are reversed. The red breast of a robin, when puffed out and thrust towards an intruding robin, is usually enough to defuse the situation and settle matters without coming to blows. Thus colours play a huge part in reducing the need for physical attacks.

If an unpaired male bird with no territory is determined to claim a space, however, fighting may ensue – robins will fight to the death. Male blackbirds will fight other male blackbirds and female blackbirds fight off female intruders.

▼ Adult gannets are vivid white: they fight and use aggressive displays in the colony. Young gannets, once they have grown out of their first covering of down, are dark to help them avoid being attacked by an adult, which could be fatal.

Young birds

Too immature to breed, young birds are not seeking either a mate or a territory, so they have no need to advertise their colours. They are better off being dull and inconspicuous. Hence we see brown-streaked young gulls and mottled brown young robins with no red breasts.

▲ Young kittiwakes have bold black marks to help distinguish them from trespassing adults.

Kittiwakes and gannets

Young kittiwakes are hatched in tiny nests on minute ledges, at a dizzy height above the sea. Above all they must not be knocked off the ledge before they can fly. If an intruding adult is at the nest, the rightful owner will attack. Adult kittiwakes have immaculate white heads. To avoid being attacked by mistake, a young one has a broad black band on its neck, which it displays to its incoming parent: 'Don't peck, it's me!'

Similarly, young gannets are blackish; adult gannets, which are pure white, are especially aggressive at their nests towards other adult gannets and a youngster must avoid being speared by another gannet's beak at all costs.

▼ Kittiwakes nest on tiny ledges above the sea.

Leaving the nest

It is a tough world for young birds once they have left the nest and become independent of their parents. Small birds, such as finches, tits and thrushes, become mature enough to breed at one year old. Those that live in flocks in the winter have an easier time, but robins, for instance, already need to carve out a territory of their own in the winter. Young robins gain their red plumage by the autumn and soon fight with adults on equal terms. Male and female robins have separate territories in winter, too, so the competition for space is especially fierce.

▲ This robin is feeding its chicks soon after they have left the nest. They are brown and mottled, with none of the adult robin's red – camouflage is more important at this age.

Postures and displays

Birds use straightforward physical actions, as well as their colours, in communicating with each other and with other species. Display is body language, or communication by posture or movement, in a stereotyped or ritual way. All displays must be 'standardized' for each species so that other individuals can recognize them and know exactly what they mean. That means you, too, can begin to read the signs.

Submissive displays

A bird in a submissive pose is saying the same thing as a dog with its tail between its legs: 'I give in, so don't hurt me'. These postures help to avoid a fight. Females use submissive poses when pairing with males, overcoming the natural tendency for any close encounter to end in a fight. Birds have their 'individual space', which is not to be invaded by other birds, but courtship has to break down such built-in barriers.

▼ Aggression is easy to see at the bird feeder: great tits (left) usually dominate smaller blue tits (right) by threatening them, without the need for a costly fight.

◄ Gannets raise their heads and tails, pointing their beaks to the sky, to indicate their intention to leave the colony and fly from the nest.

Ritualized displays

Go to a seabird colony on a cliff and watch the comings and goings of gulls, guillemots, puffins and gannets. Their lives are ruled by stereotyped, ritualized actions: precise displays each with their own meaning. Fulmars greet each other at the nest with widely gaping beaks, waved heads and guttural calls. Puffins tap bills, wave their heads, or waddle with exaggerated steps to their burrows. Such displays may reduce aggression within a tight-packed community, or reinforce pair bonds, which are essential for the successful rearing of a family in many species. Few birds will normally allow another bird to touch them: they like to keep their own space. Yet, to breed, they must be able to come together in an intimate way, to feed each other and their chicks. They have to develop trust and, at least for a few weeks, a strong bond between male and female.

MUST KNOW

Threat displays

You can easily see birds' displays, even from the kitchen window. One kind is a simple threat: 'Come closer and I'll peck you'. Great and blue tits on a feeder use threat postures, squabbling with their wings drooped, heads thrust forward and beaks open.

House sparrows

Male house sparrows add weight to their plumage patterns (the one with the biggest black bib is most likely to win a mate) by their postures. They have little in the way of song, but scuttle over the ground with head up, tail raised, body pressed down and wings half-spread, to impress watching females.

Blackbirds

Courting blackbirds are undemonstrative, but pairs get on together with little display. The male is dominant outside the breeding season, but this is reversed during summer. An unpaired male, advertising his availability to a female, will stretch upwards, bow down in a curiously 'broken' pose, or raise his rump feathers into a hump above the flattened tail. The female shows she's ready to mate by pointing her head and tail steeply upwards: a 'soliciting' posture.

▲ Here is a male house sparrow in spring, his black bib at its most extensive. He looks fit, strong and a suitable father for healthy chicks, so a female might select him instead of a male with a smaller bib.

Robins

Robins develop a pair bond partly by 'courtship feeding'. A male robin will feed his mate many times each day, reinforcing the bond between them and, at the same time, giving her vital extra nutrition at a time when she is forming a clutch of large, energy-packed eggs.

▼ A robin uses its red breast as a warning to other robins, intimidating them by cocking its tail, raising its head and swaying the puffed-out red chest from side to side.

Pied wagtails

Male pied wagtails occupy territories before females. In late winter or spring, a female will try to move in on the territory of a male. At first, he sees her off. The female tries again, using an 'appeasement display', with tail raised and chin up, and a special call. Over a few days the male is less likely to attack. The display is most frequent when the two first meet on the territory each morning. In spring, the male sings and bows or bobs to the female. He may display with the wing nearest the female drooped and the far wing and tail raised. Bowing and springy, leggy bouncing by the male precedes mating.

Dunnocks

These birds have complicated lives. The most obvious displays are aggressive, with rump feathers raised, body plumage ruffled and wings quickly flicked or waved momentarily, both together or one at a time. Sometimes three or four or more dunnocks move about in a bush or shrubbery, waving their wings for several minutes. Fighting is unusual for most of the year but two males competing for a single female can fight to the death.

▲ This male pied wagtail is carrying food for his chicks; a female would be greyer on the back, less sharply black and white than this. The bold white wing patches and tail sides are more clearly exposed in display postures.

MUST KNOW

Wagtails

In winter, you may see a different wagtail on the local park lake or even in a town or city. Grey wagtails visit water of any kind, even rainwater puddles on flat roofs. Their calls are higher and sharper than those of pied wagtails. Look for the patch of yellow under the longer, thinner tail.

Size

It is hard to judge a bird's size. Most things naturally look bigger at close range, but often what seems to be a 'big bird' far away becomes quite small when it is seen close up. Common garden birds such as blue tits are really tiny, while a goldcrest would fit in the palm of your hand, so it's not surprising that you may struggle to see details from 50 yards.

MUST KNOW

Big or small
Birds are usually chicken-sized or even smaller, and few are goose-sized or above. Giants in Europe include the white storks, white-tailed eagles, griffon and great bustards, which have wing spans well in excess of the height of a tall man. The smallest are the goldcrest and firecrest, both smaller than a blue tit.

Weight versus length

The common measure of size in identification books is the measurement from bill tip to tail tip, which gives little idea of bulk. A very slim, long-billed bird, such as a greenshank, is the same length as a short-billed, heavily-built one, such as a red grouse, but will look much smaller. A great black-backed gull is a few centimetres longer than a lesser black-backed gull, but may be so much more heavily built that, side by side, it looks 'twice as big'. Weight is often a better clue than length as appearances can be deceptive.

► While a wren is the same length as a goldcrest, its rounded form means that it is perhaps twice as heavy.

Big birds

These are generally more relaxed, using much less energy, eating large meals at long intervals (such as the vultures and eagles) or constantly swallowing large amounts of low-nutrition food, as do the geese, which are among the few grazers of grass and leaves.

Small birds

Many small birds live frenetic lives, really living on their nerves: they have a fast heartbeat, a high body temperature and a high metabolic rate. Such short-lived, high-speed creatures are not suited to being a very large size: they need a constant intake of food just to keep them going.

▲ A typical large bird of prey with broad wings and tail, the honey buzzard can soar effortlessly, but when it is migrating, it needs to fly over land as much as possible and to take the shortest sea crossing. It relies on warm, rising air to keep it aloft, which occurs only over land.

Shapes

These are associated with lifestyles and habitats. In the case of wildfowl, ducks, geese and swans are broad-bodied, boat-shaped birds, with a natural double-bend to the head and neck so the neck is erect and the head horizontal.

Swans

These large birds feed on submerged vegetation and, to reach it, need their long necks. They also 'upend' with head thrust even deeper into water and tail upright, held in position by paddling their broadly-webbed feet. They graze on dry land, but are big, heavy, plodding birds with short legs, so they are not very agile and have no real need to be. They take off from water with a short run across the surface, pattering with their feet.

Geese

These are more terrestrial than swans, walking more easily on longer legs, and grazing or pecking at roots and leaves with their stouter beaks. They have medium-length, sinuous necks to

▼ The long neck of a mute swan allows it to reach food on the bottom, even in quite deep water, especially if it 'upends', with its tail in the air, reaching down to a metre or more.

◀ The shelduck is a sort of halfway-house between a duck and a goose: quite large and long-legged, with a broad, rounded bill which is specifically designed to hoover up tiny crustaceans from mud in a side-to-side sweeping action.

help them do this but have no need for the very long, slender necks that swans have. They take off much more easily than swans, with a direct leap from land or a short patter across water.

Ducks

Ducks come in several sub-groups. Some have broad, flat bills, with fine filters along each side, which are designed to sieve seeds and tiny creatures from a 'soup' of muddy water: these are the 'dabbling' ducks. They can upend, but rarely dive; some, such as the familiar mallard, also graze quite happily on land, being the 'all-rounders' of the duck world.

Others, such as the goldeneye and scoters, have deeper bills, with which they crunch small shellfish and crustaceans. Tufted ducks and pochards have broader bills for coping with small molluscs and plant material. Goosanders and mergansers have longer bills with a sharp hook at the tip and serrated edges, which are made for dealing with slippery fish. All of these feed underwater, diving under from the surface: they are 'diving ducks'.

MUST KNOW

Garden birds
Blackbirds and thrushes are 'all round' birds with quite heavy bodies, longish tails and strong legs. They can hop, run and perch in trees but can't hang upside down. Blue tits have box-like bodies and stubby legs with strong toes, ideal for hanging onto thin twigs but not so good on the ground. Dunnocks have long legs and slim toes for hopping on the ground and perching but not for clinging upside down on feeders or twigs.

▲ The long bill of this snipe is flexible and sensitive at the tip, making it ideal for probing deeply and for grasping food in soft mud.

Wading birds

Another large group shaped by lifestyle is the wading birds, including plovers and sandpipers. Most are waterside birds, feeding in muddy places or in or beside shallow water. The length of their legs and bills helps define their roles and the food that they concentrate on.

Long bills

Curlews have very long, down-curved bills, which they can use to probe into crevices for crabs or to push deep into soft mud for marine worms and earthworms. Godwits concentrate on worms in tidal mud, using their straight or even slightly upcurved bills for probing.

Snipe do the same in muddy places by freshwater: they have sensitive and flexible bill tips that can not only feel worms but also open slightly: they can grab and swallow a worm underground. While they are doing this, they need to be aware of potential danger: snipes and woodcocks have large eyes set so far back on their heads that they can see behind them while they feed. With their specialist detection equipment, probing deep into the ground, they have no need to look forwards.

Shorter bills

Knots, dunlins, common sandpipers and many other waders have shorter bills, but they are still quite long and thin; they pick from the surface, or probe with quick, shallow pin-pricks, taking tiny food from the surface of mud or just below it.

The plovers are even shorter-billed. The ringed plover picks its food from the ground without probing. The turnstone has a thicker bill, flat on top and slightly upcurved beneath, ideal for slipping beneath pebbles and lumps of stranded seaweed, which are tossed over to reveal tiny insects and crustaceans hiding underneath.

▲ The long bill of a curlew is a tool for probing in mud, while the shorter bills of the grey plovers and knots alongside are made for picking food from the surface of mud and sand.

◄ The avocet has a remarkable beak: it is swept upwards and flattened towards the tip, so that, as the bird leans forwards, it can be swept sideways just below the surface of salty water or semi-liquid mud.

Unusual birds

The black-winged stilt is closely related to the avocet but does things differently. Its enormously long legs mean it can wade into deeper water, but has a shorter, straight bill for picking insects from the surface with delicacy and precision.

Beaks

Beaks (or bills) are used for several tasks, such as preening ('zipping' the vanes of disarranged feathers back together and removing dust and feather mites), drinking and building nests. Their principal day-to-day use, however, is feeding, and it is this that shapes them.

Unusual bills

Some European birds have remarkable bills. The greater flamingo has an angled one so that when the tall, long-necked bird holds its head into water, the bill is upside down, the 'upper' half becoming a deep, boat-shaped scoop, the 'lower' half a flat 'lid'. Water is taken into the bill and pumped out by the muscular tongue through a network of fine mesh, trapping food inside. The mush of tiny food items is then forced down by the broad, muscular tongue. Pelicans have famously large bills with flexible pouches that can scoop up large volumes of water, which is then expelled, while the bird hangs on tightly to any fish that it has caught.

◄ A pelican uses its large bill to scoop up water and fish into its soft, extendable pouch. It squeezes out the water and swallows the fish.

Hooked bills

Birds of prey have hooked bills, to help tear up prey. Falcons have a 'tooth' or notch, on the edge of the upper mandible, to help dispatch prey with a strong nip to the neck. Most birds of prey kill with their feet and use their bills for feeding.

▲ The falcon's bill has a distinctive hooked tip, which makes it useful for tearing its prey into bite-size bits.

Other bills

● Warblers have slim bills to probe into foliage and pick up fragile insects.
● Flycatchers have broader beaks, fringed with stiff bristles to snap up insects in flight.
● Swallows have small bills, but extremely wide mouths which help catch insects in mid-air.
● Blackbirds have stouter beaks which are used for pulling up worms or probing for insects amongst leaf litter, but are also tough enough to pluck berries and break into fallen apples.
● Finches' bills tend to be triangular and stout to deal with strong seeds, but they vary greatly.
● Redpolls have tiny, short bills.
● Siskins have longer ones for picking out the seeds from cones.
● Goldfinches have still longer, fine-tipped beaks, perfect for getting into cones and teasels.
● Greenfinches have stouter bills, with sharp edges to help de-husk large seeds and grains.

▲ Treecreepers have fine, downcurved bills, which are ideal for probing into bark for small insects.

Legs and feet

Legs and feet vary just as much as beaks. Most birds have a standard three toes forward, one back pattern, but a few, such as the fast-running sanderlings, have just three toes. Leg length also varies greatly, from the tiny, almost useless legs of the swift, with four tiny forward-facing toes, to the enormously long ones of flamingos and stilts.

Swimming birds

Mostly, these have webbed feet. Ducks' feet have three toes joined by webs and a free hind toe, but cormorants and gannets have all four toes webbed. Coots, grebes and divers have a different foot, with their toes broadly lobed. When swimming, the lobes are wide open to present the greatest possible thrust on the back stroke, but on the forward stroke they fold back, closed to minimize drag.

▼ Although large and heavy, the eider duck is quite streamlined and has webbed feet, which are ideal for swimming in the sea and underwater.

◀ Cormorants, like gannets, have all their four toes connected by broad webs, giving them additional propulsion when swimming and diving underwater.

Wading birds

These birds have long, fine toes, which are useful for spreading the bird's weight on soft mud. Moorhens have particularly long toes, helping them to walk on floating vegetation. They do not need the broad lobes of the coot, as they seldom dive deeply for food and they swim much less often.

▼ The moorhen is a good all-rounder, swimming, climbing and walking, and its long toes are particularly suited for spreading its weight on semi-floating vegetation in ponds.

Birds of prey

These birds have strong, muscular, tough-scaled feet. Their toes have sharp, curved claws, or talons, for holding and killing prey. However, not all conform to this basic pattern. The honey buzzard digs out wasps' nests and has short toes with blunt claws; vultures do not kill and have short legs but long toes, and claws that are not especially sharp. Ospreys have stubby toes equipped with sharp scales, to help them grasp slippery fish, and huge, arched claws. They can reverse the outer toe, so that, instead of having the usual pattern of three forward, one back, they have two forward, two back (or one to the side) to give a better grip.

▲ Precision and power allow the white-tailed eagle to pinpoint a dead or floating fish and dive down to pick it up with its feet. Its broad wings give it plenty of lift to fly up after its dive.

▼ An osprey has short, powerful toes but extremely long, hooked claws and spiky scales on the soles of its feet, to give extra grip on a slippery fish.

Other birds

Woodpeckers and owls also have two toes forward, two toes back: this 'zygodactyl' pattern is also shown by the cuckoo. Kingfishers have two toes fused at the based, to help them shovel loose earth backwards as they burrow their long nesting tunnels. Puffins do the same thing and have the inner claw sharp and incurved to help them dig.

Songbirds with three forward toes and one hind toe have special tendons that help them to grip a perch as they rest their weight upon it and flex the leg. Those that run through long grass, such as the meadow pipit and skylark, tend to have very long hind claws.

▲ The outer toe of this lesser spotted woodpecker is turned backwards, so as to provide a wider, stronger grip on curved branches and tree trunks.

Calls and song

Not only are birds' plumage patterns surprisingly constant, according to their species, age, season and sex, but each species has characteristic calls, or vocalizations, which help us to identify them. They are distinctive because, in most cases, they are intended to communicate something to other individuals of the same species, and therefore they must be recognizably different from other species' sounds.

Alarm calls

Some calls are specific to males, females or young birds, in the same way that each has its own plumage. Most birds will have several calls and usually one or two can be recognized easily while others may be confusingly difficult to identify: these are typically 'alarm calls', which warn of approaching danger.

Alarm calls given by small woodland birds are high-pitched and thin, with no strong consonant sounds – a simple 'sseeeee'. This penetrating sound can be heard within a wood, warning of the approach of a sparrowhawk perhaps, but the lack of hard elements makes it extremely difficult to pinpoint. The bird can give the call without revealing its position to the hawk. Hard-ended notes are more easily located.

Contact calls

Other bird calls (or 'notes') include 'contact calls' which help families or winter flocks or migrating groups to stay together. They are more or less 'conversational', and are given every so often to reassure others: 'I'm still here', or 'follow me'.

Typical contact calls are short and simple, such as the hard 'tak' of a blackcap and the short, dry trill of a long-tailed tit. Calm October nights, just after dark, are pierced by the 'seeee' calls of migrating redwings.

▲ A singing robin is usually saying: 'This is my territory, so keep out'.

MUST KNOW

Gravel pits
Gravel pits and their environs are often good places to see woodland birds as well as wildfowl and waders and to listen to their calls. Birds of prey may also be close by. No wonder some gravel pit complexes have become favourites of birdwatchers across the UK and Europe.

Flight calls

Contact calls merge into flight calls, which are obviously given in flight and very handy for our bird recognition. A chaffinch calls a simple 'chup' whereas a greenfinch has a more complex twitter, a redpoll a harder, more metallic trill.

Wading birds have especially distinctive flight calls, which are vital in identification: the ringed plover's 'too-ip' compared with the short 'pew' of a little ringed plover; the curlew's 'cur-lee' and the whimbrel's rapid 'tip-ip-ip-ip-ip-ip-ip-ip'; the rich, yodelling 'chuwee-wee-wee' of the green sandpiper compared with the sharp, quick 'chif-if-if' of the similar wood sandpiper. Such calls from waders convey alarm, too, when they are given in a louder, more intense form.

▲ Oystercatchers have loud, piercing calls, easily heard over long distances above the rush of wind and waves on the seashore.

◀ A curlew's alarm call warns its chicks, or other curlews, that danger is near. However, it also helps us to locate the bird.

MUST KNOW

Young birds
Young birds call to be fed: listen for baby blackbirds with their deep, purring trills, or young blue tits calling with sharp, feeble-sounding but penetrating sounds. Adults give warning calls to make their chicks keep stock still. Male birds of prey call to a female on the nest to say 'I'm coming in, with food'.

▼ Not very musical, but still a song, the characteristic call of the corncrake is a sharp, double rasp.

Bird song

Song is the most complex and developed kind of vocal communication. Most species have a distinct song that we can learn with practice. Some are simple and stereotyped, whereas others are more complex but also with little individual variation. Yet others, such as the song of a blackbird or nightingale, maintain the recognizable character of the species but involve individual improvisation and great variety.

The repetitive, harsh, double rasp of a corncrake is a 'song' in terms of its function, but it is not in the least musical – bird song is not necessarily musical in a human sense. It lets other birds know that the singer is there. In territorial species, other males know that the territory is occupied.

At the same time, even in the more colonial species, such as the linnet, females are attracted to the song of a male. Linnets will also gather together sometimes and will perform a kind of communal chorus of cheerful song.

◄ Skylarks often sing from posts but they are at their best when they are singing from high up in the air in a special song flight.

When to hear song

Song is especially concentrated early in the day and again at dusk – in spring and early summer the famous 'dawn chorus' in a woodland is unforgettable. However, birds will often sing throughout the day and sometimes even at night. Robins sing beneath street lights in industrial areas and beside car parks at night, and are often taken for nightingales. Birds often surprise us: I've listened to goldcrests singing at dawn from conifers encased in thick hoar frost when surely they should be spending every moment finding food.

Copying sounds

Song is largely inherited, but in the best songsters it is also partly learned, or copied. For example, the marsh warbler, an astonishingly good mimic, may include in its song the calls and song of scores of birds that it hears during the winter in Africa, as well as a dozen or more from other species around it in the summer in Europe.

Blackbirds add phrases from others nearby and also sometimes copy artificial sounds, such as telephones and even car alarms. Increased complexity tells others that this is a mature, experienced, fit bird, not to be trifled with – and potentially a father of strong, healthy offspring.

▼ Song thrushes are typical of those birds that sing regularly from a number of perches around their breeding territories.

Learning bird calls

It is best to learn a few bird songs in winter when fewer species are singing and thus there is less confusion. With fewer trees in leaf, they are easier to see, too. Blackbirds, song and mistle thrushes, and robins all sing early in the year. Later, the simple two-note repetitions of great tits, the fast, slightly flat warble of a dunnock, the cheerful rattle of a chaffinch and the loud, energetic song of the wren join in.

Try to track down each sound as you hear it so that you can fix both sound and sight in your memory: it is easier learning songs by hearing the real thing and watching the bird that creates it than by listening to tapes and CDs. But these help reinforce your mental images and are better than descriptions in a book, such as 'chip-ip-ip-tee-oo', which really make sense only as reminders, when you know the sound already.

Calls can be harder, and many are confusingly alike at first. The subtle differences between the sharp, high-pitched 'seee-seee-seee' of a goldcrest and the shriller, more metallic 'seee-seee-sees' of a long-tailed tit will only stay in your mind with experience.

▲ Marsh warblers are best told from reed warblers by their remarkable, musical songs with imitations of dozens of other birds' calls incorporated within them.

◄ Blackbirds have mellow, fluty songs, which are more flowing than the repetitive songs of song thrushes.

Start with familiar birds

Initiate yourself by learning the calls of the birds in your garden, on your way to work or school. Perhaps you will add the sharp 'chissik' of a pied wagtail, the triple coo and slurred flight note of a collared dove, or the squeaky 'chak' of a jackdaw to your list of easily remembered bird sounds. A town park lake will increase these considerably, with the familiar quack of a mallard, the loud, sharp exclamations from moorhens and coots, and the squeal of black-headed gulls.

Use descriptive terms, such as 'squeal', 'shout', 'sharp', 'metallic' and 'mellow', to try to describe the sounds you hear. Write them down if you can - even peculiar notations ('week', 'swairnk', 'tiki-tiki-too') help to fix sounds in your mind. You might draw a line above the word, rising and falling over each syllable to show any variation in pitch – anything to help you remember. Once you know sounds, you will react to them. The hard 'tink tink' of a starling is a special alarm warning of a sparrowhawk, which you can use to help you spot the hawk, too.

▲ Even wading birds on the beach each have distinctive calls that help us to identify them in flight.

want to know more?

Take it to the next level...

Go to...
▶ **Habitats for birds** – page 116
▶ **Use your records** – page 182
▶ **Join a club** – page 186

Other sources
▶ **CDs and DVDs**
   for top-quality bird song recordings
▶ **Bird magazines**
   look for ads for bird song tapes
▶ **Bird song tapes**
   for playing in the car on long journeys
▶ **Field guides**
   for illustrations of bird shapes, etc.
▶ **Publications**
   visit www.collins.co.uk for Collins bird books

habitats

for birds

You will soon notice that while certain birds live in particular areas near you, they do not live elsewhere – each species has its own favoured habitat. A habitat is defined as the sum of the characteristics of the area in which a bird lives, including the vegetation, nest sites, roosting sites, food and feeding areas, as well as the weather and the altitude.

What is a habitat?

Many species are generalists and can make a living in a surprising variety of places. Even so, they have their special needs and, if these are lost, they disappear. Others are specialists and it is much easier to see how they are tied to a particular habitat and way of life.

A means of survival

A bird's habitat is a complete summary of the kind of places where it lives and which supply all it needs to survive. Take the house sparrow, for instance. It lives in towns, suburbs, villages, gardens, farms and farmland, and it is usually associated with people. Look more closely and it seems to need holes in walls and buildings, sometimes in trees, to nest in, although it can make its untidy ball of grass and wool in a thick hedge or some ivy.

▼ House sparrows seem to be at home anywhere and everywhere, but in fact they are strongly connected with places where people live.

It also needs water, and it likes to take a dust bath, so it may prefer places with loose, light soils. And it must be able to dash to the cover of a thick hedge or some shrubbery when danger threatens. Sparrows like to sit in such thickets and twitter their communal songs; they need dense vegetation of some sort to sleep in at night.

Threats to habitat

It seems, at first, that house sparrows can live anywhere – they are real opportunists. But, on closer examination, they have particular needs. If a farmer is forced to keep birds out of his grain stores, the sparrows will suffer. If combine harvesters are more efficient and spill less grain than the traditional harvesting methods, and gardeners stop growing vegetables and replace weedy corners with decking, sparrows have less to eat and they will subsequently decline. If we put PVC cladding on eaves and soffits, tidy up the brickwork and block holes in our roofs, there are fewer places for sparrows to nest. In many areas, changes to their habitat and food supplies have led to sparrows disappearing altogether.

▲ Sparrows use dust baths to help rid their plumage of parasites; a good dusting area is just one requirement in an ideal habitat.

▼ A house sparrow also needs plenty of seeds to eat, and insects too when it is feeding its chicks. So, it needs the right kind of plants; in late summer, there used to be flocks of hundreds of house sparrows in ripening wheat fields.

◄ Dippers are found only near water. They nest under banks overhanging water and feed alongside and under the water; without it, they cannot survive.

Specialist habitats

If the habitats of the generalists can disappear, what about those of the specialists? The dipper is a unique songbird that wades into water, swims on the surface and even dives underneath. It uses its long, sharp claws to get a grip on the bottom and leans forward so the flow of the stream pushes it down. Its diet exploits the abundance of insect larvae and crustaceans in freshwater streams – food that is out of reach of most birds.

It has to have running fresh water, preferably with a few overhanging trees and stony shallows where it can perch on a boulder. It makes its nest under an overhang above the water. Take it out of this environment and the dipper is lost: it can't feed in any other way.

Similarly, the treecreeper searches tree bark for insects and makes a good living at it, but it really cannot do much else. Now and then one may forage on a rocky outcrop or an old stone wall, but basically the treecreeper clings to bark, using its tail as a prop, creeps upwards in a spiral, then flies to the foot of the next tree and starts again. It has long, needle-sharp, arched claws, a stiff tail and a fine, curved bill that are all ideal for the job, but it is practically unable to stand or walk on level ground.

MUST KNOW

Demanding habitats

Species that have adapted to live in demanding habitats may not be able to live elsewhere. While a sparrow can perch in a tree or hop about on the ground, a reed warbler is at home in the dense stems of tall reeds. It grasps these upright perches and hops from reed to reed but can't walk easily on flat ground nor make its nest in a loose bush. A bird that has adapted to a demanding habitat cannot go back.

Dependence on habitat

Birds' dependence on a specific habitat is absolute. Understanding such relationships is the basis of conservation. Blue tits eat seeds and insects, and they must have holes to nest in. In spring, they have just one large brood of young, which is timed to coincide with the abundance of green caterpillars on woodland trees. If their timing is wrong, their chicks starve.

▲ Blue tits are woodland birds that have coped very well with the transition of much of our woodland to garden habitats.

Barn owls

These thrive in grassy places with an abundance of small rodents. They eat mice, voles, rats and shrews but very little else. Intensive farmland, which is cultivated right up to the edge of every field, with hedges grubbed out and no grassy field margins, is hopeless for barn owls. There are no small rodents in prairies of winter wheat.

The barn owl needs somewhere to nest, too: a big hole in an old tree, a cavity in a wall or a broad beam inside a barn. Barn owls like to roost in separate holes and rest for a time during the night in such cavities, so a pair needs several holes scattered around a large territory, and patches of rough, unkempt grass where they can hunt. If the grass is too long, they cannot see the mice or get through it to catch them.

▼ Many areas of grass that are just the right length are found alongside roads, which are lethal places for barn owls, and they may easily end up as the victims of passing traffic.

Bitterns

These are brilliantly adapted to live in tall, dense reeds above water, using their huge toes to cling to reed stems or balance their weight as they lean forward, looking for fish. However, any old reedbed will not do – well camouflaged as they are, bitterns do not like to come out into the open and they prefer to feed on the edge of a reedbed or well hidden inside it. They cannot come out into open water to find fish: the fish have to come to them.

So a good reedbed for a bittern must be wet enough to allow fish to swim inside, or have narrow ditches of open water overshadowed by tall banks of reed. Reedbeds have a natural tendency to dry out and turn into bushy scrub, and to keep bitterns in the modern world, where new floods and reedbeds are unlikely to take the place of old ones as they dry out, we have to maintain healthy, wet reedbeds by expensive management and manipulation of water tables.

▼ Bitterns must have reedbeds; when they stand still and stretch themselves upright, they even look like a bunch of reeds.

◀ In the early years of the twenty-first century, many guillemots have found it harder to find food, such as sandeels, and in some years many colonies have failed to rear any young. Their relationship with the sea and its abundance of fish has changed drastically, probably because of rapid climate change.

Complex relationships

The more that birds are studied, the more complex their relationships with their habitats, including their food supplies, are found to be. Even seabirds, which simply go to sea to find fish and nest on cliffs on the coast, have complex relationships with water temperatures, plankton, fish populations and other factors that together make up or influence the intricate web of life in the ocean. As the North Sea is warming up, so the plankton is moving north. Sand eels that feed on plankton move north, too; at the same time, sand eels are being grossly overfished by humans. A shortage of sand eels plus overfishing means a dangerous decline in the numbers of predatory fish, such as cod. It also means that fulmars, kittiwakes, arctic terns and guillemots are unable to find enough food to breed successfully. In the first decade of the twenty-first century, many of these birds are having their worst breeding seasons on record.

MUST KNOW

Food webs
Birds can thrive only if their complicated food webs are also thriving. These may start with just tiny organisms in the soil, which are devoured by small insects, then larger insects, or soil nutrients that allow plants to grow which produce food for insects and set seed. The seedbank in the soils of much of our farmland has been depleted by intensive farming and modern fields can be almost devoid of bird life.

Changes in habitat

Birds have to find enough to eat, day after day, in the small area in which they live. They need nest sites, roosting sites and safe places to hide when they are threatened. Take away any of these and most birds are unable to cope. They have been adapting to specialized ways of living for millions of years and they cannot change now.

Changes in farmland

In eastern England, there used to be vast open areas, where small songbirds of woodlands and woodland edges were absent. Then came the enclosures, weaving a network of hedgerows over such regions, and in came the thrushes, finches, warblers and many other birds that thrived on what, earlier, were hostile areas for them. But birds of the open fields, such as stone-curlews, lapwings and skylarks, lost out.

Nevertheless, many areas had a traditional patchwork of field types, with ploughed ground, fallow, crops and orchards creating richly varied environments. Lapwings could nest on grass but feed their chicks on bare earth. Skylarks nested in short grass grazed down by stock.

▲ Farmland habitats have always changed but only in recent decades has such change been so fast and so dramatic that birds have been affected severely. Fields of wheat and barley stubble, left all winter after harvesting and full of seeds for hungry birds, are now rarely seen.

A greater concentration on wheat and a loss of dairy and beef farming changed this. Skylarks still nested in fields of cereals sown in spring, but lapwings were restricted in this more uniform environment. In the west, lapwings still bred in fields where small numbers of cattle and sheep grazed, but as farming intensified, they were squeezed out by overgrazing.

Spring sowing meant crops were still short in the nesting season; after the harvest, stubble was left all winter, providing spilled grain and weed seed for larks, finches and buntings. Then came combine harvesting and the loss of stackyards, so spilled grain was scarce.

Autumn sowing changed everything: cereal crops became tall and thick by early spring, and neither lapwings nor skylarks could feed or nest in them. The fields were ploughed in autumn and re-seeded, doing away with winter stubble, so there was nothing to eat through the winter.

Modern intensification has been so fast that many farmland birds are now rare and unable to cope, just like many of the farmland plants, or 'weeds', that used to be so abundant.

Yellowhammers
These have become much scarcer in recent years: in Northern Ireland they have practically disappeared. They need insects in spring for their chicks, and seeds in winter for survival, but neither food is now easy to find.

▼ Leaving small patches of unseeded ground in fields of cereals does very little to reduce the farmer's income, but helps skylarks to survive in an otherwise increasingly hostile habitat.

Changing habitats

Migration can help many species to cope with the demands of survival. Wading birds can feed on the abundance of tiny worms, molluscs and crustaceans in the mud of an estuary, where there may be tens of thousands of minute organisms in a square metre of surface mud, enriched twice a day by the incoming tides. They spread out to feed as the tide recedes, but must withdraw as the water rises and move off to a safe place to roost during the high tide period.

This pattern varies during each month according to the level of the tides: spring tides cover even the highest parts of the beach and make feeding impossible, while neap tides leave so much exposed that the birds may continue feeding all day. High tides also occur at any time of day and night, so waders must be able to feed at dusk and dawn or even at night, or by day – they have to adapt to changing circumstances.

However, most cannot breed here. Some lapwings and redshanks do nest on high, safe saltmarshes, but most must move at least to open moors and upland fields, or to lowland

MUST KNOW

The seasons
Great movements of millions of birds across the surface of the earth have been stimulated by the changing seasons. Opportunities exist in the north in summer, which birds have taken advantage of, but in winter, they have to move south to avoid severe conditions: they depend on 'empty' habitats in Africa.

▼ Wading birds breed in the far north and winter south as far as Africa: they must have rich feeding and safe refuges on their migration routes between the two.

HABITATS FOR BIRDS

pastures. The great majority of the winter waders in western Europe fly off to the Arctic, to breed on the tundra as soon as conditions there allow, which may not be until June. They and their growing chicks feed on millions of summer insects, mostly midges and their larvae in the shallow pools.

▲ Dunlins breeding in Scotland may nest on high moors or mountain tops, in sub-arctic conditions, or low down in rich pastureland close to the sea.

Contrasting habitats

The birds mentioned above have quite different habitats according to the season, and some of the same species may have various habitats that differ greatly from each other. Oystercatchers, for example, may breed on northern shores, rocky islets, shingle beaches, or in riverside fields far inland.

The swift is a remarkable bird whose habitat is essentially open air, for most of its life. It feeds and even sleeps in the air for many months of the year, flying over Africa, and crossing much of Europe on migration. For a brief period it needs access to shaded cavities in rocks, trees or (almost exclusively now) buildings in which to nest, rather like a seabird that has to come to land to breed.

Gardens and parks

Most of us have access to a garden of some sort or to a town park. These attract woodland-edge birds that have adapted to a way of life close to people, often supported by people who put out food, deliberately or unwittingly, and nestboxes.

▲ Recently, great spotted woodpeckers have greatly increased as visitors to our garden feeders.

Location matters

What you see depends on where you are. Some garden visitors are regulars in mainland Europe but not in the UK (such as black woodpeckers and firecrests), or are found in small parts of the UK but not elsewhere (such as the crested tit). Others, such as great spotted woodpeckers and tawny owls, are not found in Ireland.

Even a window ledge is enough for a town pigeon, descendant of the wild rock dove. It might attract house sparrows, too, which are less abundant but still widespread in most towns and suburbs, if there is still enough food and somewhere for them to nest inside a cavity. A hanging feeder beside a window will sometimes tempt blue tits to feed high up on a block of flats.

Gardens

Even a moderate-sized garden with just a lawn, a flowerbed, a shrubbery and a bird table will bring in quite a variety of birds.

Robins

The robin has learned to exploit people, having adapted to following animals, such as wild boars, rooting about in woods. Now it snatches insects, worms and centipedes which are upturned by gardeners' spades.

Blue and great tits

These feed eagerly at tables and feeders and nest in garden boxes, but, as there is usually far less natural food in spring, rear fewer young than in the woods. Close to woods, garden-watchers can expect to see coal tits, but marsh and willow tits are scarce. Long-tailed tits have begun to feed on garden feeders and are now regulars in some places although still unknown in others.

Pied wagtails

Pied (on the continent, white) wagtails feed not only on larger lawns but also on areas of tarmac and concrete, catching insects; they nest in outbuildings or woodpiles. A nesting bird that is very rare in the UK, but common in many towns in Europe, is the black redstart, which is also at home around large buildings that replicate the natural cliffs and rocks of its original habitat.

Wrens, dunnocks, blackbirds and thrushes

These little birds seek insects at the foot of the shrubbery and add interest with their songs. Typical songsters also include two birds that feed on the lawn: the blackbird and song thrush. Song thrushes used to be the commoner of the two, but now it is usually the blackbird that is most abundant and creates the greater part of the spring dawn chorus.

▲ Blue tits are typical of the birds that are attracted to artificial feeding stations.

▼ Greenfinches and robins eagerly feed on birdtables topped with seed mixtures and kitchen scraps.

Starlings

These are common in many gardens, increasing in autumn and winter. They often bring their newly fledged families to feed on lawns: unkempt lawns where there might be leatherjackets and other grubs are best. They sing from television aerials and rooftops with their characteristically drooped wings and rattling, crackling repertoire. In Spain and Portugal, they are replaced by a different species, the spotless starling.

▲ Starlings have greatly declined in much of Europe, but still remain frequent visitors, albeit in reduced numbers, to many gardens.

Doves and woodpigeons

Another bird singing from the TV aerial will be the collared dove: widespread and often common. The much bigger woodpigeon has become increasingly tame in many gardens, coming to birdtables and also eating buds, flowers and berries of shrubs such as elder.

House martins, swifts and swallows

Feeding above rooftop level, house martins build round nests of mud under eaves. Swifts nest inside older house roofs and other old buildings such as church towers, if holes are not blocked. Swallows, which fly lower, close to the ground, often nest around farms. They prefer open countryside to gardens.

Magpies, crows and jackdaws

Magpies scavenge for scraps all year and eat an abundance of insects and grubs in summer. They also take eggs and nestlings and are unwelcome in most gardens, but spectacular to look at: they are often disliked as much for the fact that they make the blackbirds call in alarm from dawn to dusk as anything else. Carrion crows are found in the suburbs where there are tall trees, and jackdaws like old buildings and trees with large cavities. They often mix with rooks at a suburban rookery.

▲ The house martin builds mud nests under the eaves; swallows prefer sheltered spots in sheds and barns.

▼ Although insectivorous for much of the year, magpies eat anything they can find.

Finches

A number of finches enjoy gardens. The chaffinch is typical, coming to feed on birdtables (or underneath, on spilled seed) and nesting in larger gardens in spring: its bright, rattling song is a delight. Greenfinches flock to feeders stocked with sunflower seeds and also eat cotoneaster and other berries: they nest in tall, old hedges or belts of conifers such as yew hedges.

In southern Europe, the serin is a frequent garden bird; in the north, it is the siskin that comes to feeders, especially in spring, attracted by peanuts (especially in red baskets) and the newly available niger (or nyjer) seed. This seed also seems to attract goldfinches like magic. They often (but not always) appear in gardens where they have never been seen before within days (even hours) of this food being offered.

The goldfinch (like the long-tailed tit) shows how even in gardens bird populations are far from static, moving up the scale from 'rare' to 'regular' inside a decade.

▲ The triangular bill and stout shape are indicative of a finch. The white wingbars indicate it is a chaffinch.

MUST KNOW

Finches

Each finch has its own place in a habitat and has adapted to fill it to perfection. Compare the stubby bill, large body and short legs of the bullfinch, which eats large, soft seeds and buds, with the long beaks of goldfinches and siskins, which probe deeply into multiple seed heads and pine cones.

◀ Tawny owls are heard more than they are seen, being strictly nocturnal in their hunting habits. They spend the day in dense ivy or high in the thick foliage of an evergreen.

Sparrowhawks and owls

Sparrowhawks often dash through gardens hoping to surprise a small bird at a feeder or on the lawn. They are much more frequent inside gardens than kestrels. Tawny owls take birds, as well as worms, mice and voles if they are around, after dark. In big gardens, they like to sit out the day in a tall evergreen oak or pine.

Parks

These have a similar range but attract some bigger birds, too, especially if there is a pond or lake. There you may see grey herons, mallards, coots and moorhens. Black-headed gulls are around almost all year and common and herring gulls may join them in winter.

▼ Suburban areas and villages have all kinds of good places for birds: any small pond or stream will attract semi-tame mallards.

Towns and cities

Urban areas can often be surprisingly good for seeing a wide range of birds. Many big cities tend to have a river running through them, with some sort of embankment or even a quay, where many birds congregate.

Town centres

These are hostile places for birds, with few sources of food other than scraps accidentally thrown aside by people. Some town centre streets at night attract tawny owls which feed on the mice and rats drawn to waste discarded around fast-food outlets, but most have only pigeons, the occasional starling and, in places, a few house sparrows and pied wagtails.

Pigeons

In town centres, most authorities try to reduce pigeon numbers. Often scruffy and undeniably messy, these birds add movement and colour to the urban scene. Tall buildings, road and railway tunnels, and underground stations make good substitutes for natural cliffs and caves for pigeons.

MUST KNOW

Untidy is best
Towns and suburbs are apt to be tidy, and open areas are often covered in short grass and ornamental shrubs – unsuitable for birds. Untidy spots with water, bushes and rough ground can be better for birds.

▼ Although pigeons make a mess, they also add life and colour to dreary streets.

Birds of prey

Increasingly, urban areas attract peregrines, which now nest in a number of cities, preying largely on pigeons and nesting on inaccessible ledges. Kestrels also nest on buildings, from tower blocks to cathedrals, and feed on small birds and mice in the streets and parks. Tawny owls emerge at night to feed on rats in the streets of many towns, especially around fast-food outlets where the assorted rubbish and discarded food scraps attract rodents.

Crows, jays and rooks

Carrion crows are town birds if they have tall trees in which to nest and an open space in which to feed without constant disturbance from people. They sometimes become bolder and feed in the streets, usually early in the morning before many people are about. In larger parks, as in London, even jays can make a living, flying unnoticed from treetop to treetop unless a passerby happens to know their screeching calls and looks up to watch one dash overhead. Rooks are less frequent in towns but they are often found in car parks at motorway services and in some town parks.

▲ Birds of prey, especially kestrels and, sometimes, even peregrines, live in our large towns and cities. They use the ledges of high buildings as safe places to roost and nest.

▼ Carrion crows are both intelligent and adaptable. They can often be seen in suburban parks and also on playing fields.

Magpies

These are clever and adaptable birds that can find food in and around skips, rubbish bins, shops, cafés in the parks and other places where people scatter litter. In many ways, we get the birds we deserve: if there is litter, there will be magpies and crows.

Swans and herons

If there is a river, mute swans are regular town centre birds. They are often fed by people, so their numbers may be higher than could be sustained by the natural food of an urban river, which is unlikely to have much vegetation along its banks. In some areas, as in the Netherlands, grey herons are remarkably bold and stand about on river banks or even beside ditches and streams between gardens, but in most they are more nervous and quick to fly off if disturbed. Nevertheless, there are enough secluded backwaters (streams, ditches and canalsides) in most towns to attract them in to catch small fish and the occasional rat.

MUST KNOW

Mute swans

These swans may be aggressive when they have young nearby. The best way to avoid any problems is to always give them a wide berth. If you have a dog, keep it on a lead. You can easily learn to recognize potential trouble as an angry swan will arch its wings, sink its head into its shoulders and will hiss loudly.

▼ Some surprising birds may be seen in urban settings, such as these lapwings and golden plovers roosting beside a car park.

▲ Herring gulls find a ready meal around fish quays, on seaside promenades and wherever people leave their rubbish and scraps.

◄ Black-headed gulls are smaller but just as bold as herring gulls. Although they do not nest in towns, they come in to feed. These two are sitting on the railings of a waterside car park.

Gulls

Black-headed gulls are lively, noisy, active scavengers and often line the roofs of riverside buildings. They dash down to the water at the first sign of food, and squabble over bread in parks and larger squares, but rarely risk a more enclosed situation such as a narrow street. The slightly larger common gull keeps to river banks and football pitches but the other kinds will sometimes come into gardens.

Other urban birds

Any area of open grass, such as a playing field, will appeal to foraging crows, starlings, blackbirds (mostly around the edges, close to a hedge in case danger threatens), gulls and pied wagtails. A surprising city centre bird in winter is the grey wagtail, which often drops in to pick insects from the edges of puddles on high, flat roofs: it is usually detected only when it flies away with a few sharp, distinctive call notes.

There may be other surprises, too. I once watched a goldcrest displaying to its reflection in a Christmas tree bauble in a town centre in December. In many towns you may suddenly hear the clamour of greylag geese flying low overhead, or the deeper honking of Canada geese. In winter, truly wild pink-footed and greylag geese often fly high over towns.

The refuse tip

Landfill sites can swarm with birds. Most now have strict rules and refuse is quickly buried under soil, but still large flocks of gulls, rooks, crows and starlings gather around them. Each time a new load of rubbish is tipped, they pile in to get what they can.

▲ We can be reminded of the wild birds living out of town, and the passing of the seasons, by flocks of geese flying overhead.

▲ Pied wagtails come to city centres every night to find a secure, warm roosting site in buildings or even trees festooned with festive Christmas lights.

For gull enthusiasts, such places are wonderful: for most people, they are appalling. The noise and smell are hardly appealing: and you must be careful regarding health and safety, and abide by the access rules. It is usually best to find the field nearby where gulls rest between bouts of feeding and try to watch them there (but these winter gull flocks can be remarkably wild and wary, often using fields in hollows that are hidden from roads and hard to approach).

Herring, lesser black-backed and black-headed gulls will be abundant, together with smaller numbers of common and great black-backed gulls. Look for yellow-legged gulls in the smaller flocks in late summer and autumn. In winter, you may be lucky enough to find a rare glaucous gull feeding for a week or two at the local tip.

▼ Landfill sites attract huge numbers of birds: starlings will feed on the insects that abound in such places, rather than on the rubbish itself, which they leave to the scavenging gulls.

Urban fringes

Unplanned urban fringes risk losing much of their wildlife value as they become 'designed' into neat and tidy country parks with cycle tracks, mown grass and spindly saplings with no undergrowth – good for people but not for birds.

Urban locations

On urban fringes are landfill sites and waste ground, often full of colourful flowers. Railway embankments and abandoned sidings host buddleia, rosebay and ragwort, attracting insects and bringing in more birds.

Bird-friendly habitats

Better for birds are urban areas with a riot of growth, ranging from nettles, thistles and brambles to jungles of buddleia, willow and hawthorn. These areas are often on old railways, abandoned industrial sites and canal sides. Avoid active railway lines and roadsides, but you can have endless fun in 'waste' places that are in reality wonderful urban nature reserves.

Gravel pits

These are often filled in, returning the mineral workings to rather poor-quality farmland, but many become lakes, which are often the focus of a country park, with a hinterland of gravelly mounds and embankments, willows and bramble brakes. Sadly, shallow pits that are, for a year or two, brilliant for waders and wildfowl, are usually made into 'attractive' lakes. The steep sides and depth of these lakes make them useless for birds.

▶ Oystercatchers may be seen around some coastal towns, especially on stony or gravelly beaches.

HABITATS FOR BIRDS

140

Waste ground

Around the pits will be the belt of 'waste' ground that has much in common with the waste of the urban fringe. Blackberries are usually everywhere, with tall grasses and other shrubs growing through in a tangle that attracts grasshopper warblers in summer. Go out on a still, sultry summer evening and listen for the unique prolonged, reeling trill of a grasshopper warbler's song. More open grassy spaces bring in meadow pipits and pied wagtails. Stonechats may appear in winter, or stay to nest if the pits are close to the milder coast. In spring, these are good spots to watch for early migrant wheatears and yellow wagtails.

▲ A surprising variety of migrant waders appear at gravel pits and muddy pools. In autumn, even a greenshank might drop by.

◀ Stonechats appear in winter on rough, heathy places and gravel pits around the urban fringe.

HABITATS FOR BIRDS

141

▲ Nightingales are confined to the south and east of Britain, where they inhabit dense thickets around gravel pits for a few years, until these become too tall.

▲ Lesser whitethroats are smart little birds, often best seen in late summer and autumn when they feed on berries before migrating south-east for the winter.

Thickets

Taller thickets become established a few years after the pits have been abandoned. In the south of the UK and much of Europe, these are ideal for nightingales. Early summer evenings may ring to the unmatched, rich, throaty notes of the nightingale's song. Also here will be blackcaps and garden warblers. Whitethroats prefer the edges of clearings and scrubby spots; lesser whitethroats the more dense, tall, ancient hedges; sedge warblers mixtures of reed mace, nettles and shrubs; and reed warblers shallow bays that grow over with reeds and reed mace, or belts of low willows that run along the shore.

Willow warblers are often as common here as they are anywhere, inhabiting mixtures of tall hawthorns, open willows and remnant patches of oak or other woodland. In well established places, where the trees are old enough to be tall and mature, you may see chiffchaffs as well as this superb list of warblers. Elders, loaded with fruit in autumn, concentrate garden warblers, blackcaps, whitethroats and lesser whitethroats as they feed up, ready for their autumn migrations.

Shallows

These are much better for birds. In summer an abundance of low growth covers gravelly islets and banks, but rising water levels in autumn kill the plants and release a vast store of seeds. This brings in startling numbers of birds, such as teal, shovelers, mallards, wigeon and other lovers of rich pickings in shallow water. If the banks are more open, even a little muddy, autumn can be an exciting time for us as common and green sandpipers, redshanks, greenshanks, ruffs, dunlins, ringed and little ringed plovers and other waders stop off to feed during their migrations.

Watch them day after day and never assume that they are the same birds on each visit. One day, even if it takes a few years, you might find something rare and totally unexpected. Good years can bring scarcer waders, including little stints and curlew and wood sandpipers.

▼ Little ringed plovers are declining in the UK. They nest on open sandy or stony ground near water, and such places are rarely left undisturbed long.

Lakes

On the water of more established lakes, often under overhanging willows and poplars, great crested grebes, coots, gadwalls and Canada geese are likely. Lakes present a great opportunity to identify and learn about ducks, and offer unrivalled close views of these really attractive birds. Go in winter to see them at their best; in high summer, you will see a mottly selection of moulting ducks, all looking dull brown.

◄ This great crested grebe has a stripey chick hitching a ride on its back. These attractive birds are often found on urban lakes.

▼ Canada geese are sometimes thought to be too common at some town lakes, but they add colour and action to many gravel pits and reservoirs.

Tufted ducks and pochards are the common diving ducks, often hauling themselves out to sleep on a sheltered bank of an undisturbed island. Cormorants are frequent and you may see them in waterside trees, perhaps with grey herons. Listen for the shrill call – and maybe the dull 'plop' – of a kingfisher as it flies away, or dives for a fish from the waterside bushes.

▲ Tufted ducks are the commonest of the 'diving ducks', which dive below the surface to feed.

WATCH OUT!

Children

Urban fringes can be exciting places for children to learn more about their birds, butterflies and wild flowers, but sadly they can also be dangerous. Watch out for broken glass and other litter, and always keep an eye on your children. However, you can enjoy the wildlife that thrives here so much more than in sanitized city parks and on garden lawns.

Farmland

Most of the open countryside is farmed in some way: from saltmarsh and open moor grazed by sheep and ponies to the most intensive crops of cereals and oilseed rape. Mixed farming is now quite scarce, but organic farming is slowly increasing. Many areas have polarized between grazing for sheep or dairy or beef cattle, and arable land, growing wheat, barley, rape and root crops – all the things we need to eat.

Farmland birds

Arable farms can still be good places for birds, especially if there are areas of set aside or wild bird cover. Winter stubble used to be a lifeline for seed-eating birds and it can still be so, attracting skylarks, tree and house sparrows, chaffinches, greenfinches, linnets, yellowhammers and corn buntings. For most of us, however, seeing mixed flocks of many hundreds of such birds on farmland is a thing of the past.

▼ Corncrakes have long been confined to the far north and west, and have greatly declined in Ireland; but a recovery has been made possible in Scotland with the co-operation of crofters and farmers.

Corncrakes

We have seen big declines in birds as varied as the corncrake, stone-curlew, redshank and tree sparrow on farmland across Europe. Corncrakes need cover early in spring, such as iris or nettle beds, and hay that hides them and their chicks right through the summer. As hayfields changed to silage (grass crops cut two or three times a season), the corncrakes were denied cover and were often killed by farm machinery. Only special schemes to encourage farmers to grow hay and cut it in ways that help the corncrakes maintain their numbers in areas such as the Hebrides.

Decline in farmland birds

Farmers have often been unfairly criticized for doing damage to wildlife when they are just responding to rules and regulations and a fiercely competitive market. It has usually been systems of subsidy and regulation that have driven intensification to such an extent that wildlife no longer has a place on many farms. Huge areas of squeaky-clean crops without a weed or an insect in sight offer nothing to birds. No wonder that farmland birds in general have declined in recent decades, often by 50 per cent or more.

▼ Skylarks are not rare, but have nevertheless declined hugely in numbers over most of the UK. Changes in farming practices have been largely to blame for this, but there are now hopeful signs that the decline can be turned around.

Ploughed land

Ploughed ground at various times of the year appeals to meadow pipits (often migrating to lower ground in autumn, from the hills where they breed). As early as June flocks of lapwings, after their short breeding season is already over, gather on ploughed ground. In late autumn and winter, lapwings and golden plovers scatter widely over such fields to feed or gather into closer flocks to rest. Watch the black-headed gulls that are usually with them. They find most of their own worms but steal many from the plovers, too: this is klepto-parasitism, a fancy name for making a living by stealing food from other birds.

Much arable land is quickly sown with new crops in the autumn and already green with fresh shoots through the winter, replacing rich winter stubbles with young cereals in fields with

▲ Lapwings are increasingly rare nesters in most of Britain, but they are still common winter visitors from the continent to open fields and marshland.

little food for birds. By the spring, the crops are dense and have already grown quite tall, removing any chance of lapwings, larks and others from nesting in them. Skylarks tend to concentrate their nests close to the 'tramlines' made by tractors and their eggs and chicks are then more vulnerable to predators. Usually, a first brood is attempted but there is no possibility of a second or third in a summer; so skylark numbers have crashed almost everywhere.

Stone-curlews also suffer from intensive use of farm machinery and the change from a patchwork of fields to a uniformity of crops. Like lapwings, they prefer some bare soil and some short grass and cannot survive in areas of tall wheat or unvaried beans or rape. But with co-operation from farmers, they still thrive in places. However, it takes a lot of work, year after year, to ensure that they do.

▲ Always restricted to southern England, the stone-curlew has declined in Britain, but conservation efforts and friendly farmers have helped to stabilize and slightly increase their numbers in recent years.

Pastoral farming

Pastoral farming has also changed with intensive stocking and the grazing of rich, improved grassland with a dense sward of just one kind of grass. Wet areas have been drained, rushy fields transformed, and tussocky meadows turned into uniform green swards. As a consequence, lapwings, curlews, redshanks, snipe, yellow wagtails and reed buntings have all found survival difficult, if not impossible.

MUST KNOW

Finding the birds

Farming shapes the nature of most of our countryside: the lowland fields with hedgerows and woods, rolling chalk downs, picturesque northern dales, open moors, and even to some extent heaths with their ponies are all farmed. Much of your birdwatching will be on farmland of some sort. There are still many gems of beautiful landscape and accessible countryside, but you may have to work harder than previous generations to find the birds.

Woodland

Woodland includes a broad range of habitat types, which
essentially involve a substantial covering of trees and shrubs.
Within it, there are: deciduous woods (which shed their leaves
in winter); coniferous woods (which largely keep their leaves
all year); and mixtures of both. Each category has subdivisions,
with forests of oak, ash, beech, pine, larch and spruce.

Old and new

There are still a few ancient forests and many
remnant patches of the old 'wildwood', but
many of our woods are quite new. Some
deciduous plantations look entirely natural to
most of us, while many conifer plantations are
obvious to all, with their regular ranks of trees of
uniform age and structure.

▼ The typical woodland
predator of small birds is
the dashing sparrowhawk.
However, it has declined
a little in line with falling
numbers of its prey.

Oak woods

A fine oak wood will, in reality, have a great variety of trees and shrubs within it, including much holly and cherry and, in most places now, introduced but long-established sycamore and sweet chestnut. Even within the UK, oak woods vary: in the west, they tend to be mainly of sessile oak, which may be tall or dwarf in nature, often overgrazed by sheep to give bare ground beneath, whereas in the south and east most are of English oak, growing into huge, broad, ancient trees. The western woods are excellent for three summer visitors – pied flycatchers, redstarts and wood warblers – which are scarce or absent in the east.

Typical widespread oak wood birds include sparrowhawks, buzzards, tawny owls (not in Ireland), great spotted woodpeckers (also absent from Ireland), dunnocks, wrens, robins, blue, great and coal tits, song thrushes, blackbirds, chaffinches and starlings.

▲ Numbers of the great spotted woodpecker have increased, perhaps partly because of the reduced competition for nest holes as starlings have declined.

MUST KNOW

Coppicing

Coppiced woodland has a thick layer at ground level, perfect for nightingales. An old style of managing woodland, coppicing involves cutting the trees down to their stumps to encourage a dense growth of tall, slender poles.

Spring

This is the best time to see and hear woodland birds, before the leaves are too dense and dark. In winter, you may need to find a feeding flock as it roams through the woodland, otherwise the woods may seem almost empty of birds.

▼ An elusive woodland bird, the hawfinch cracks open large seeds with its bill.

Mixed woodland

Wood warblers like a thick canopy but plenty of open space underneath the trees, so they are also common in some beech woods, whose dark shade encourages such conditions. Beech woods (especially if they have hornbeams and cherries) are also good for the increasingly rare hawfinch, as well as commoner (but declining) marsh tits and, in most areas, (although not in Scotland) nuthatches.

Some large, ancient, mixed forests, adjacent to parkland or extensive heaths, have rare honey buzzards as well as common buzzards. Woodland near heaths, open farmland and flooded pits are good for hobbies, which eat dragonflies and small, aerial birds, while the main daytime predator inside the wood is the sparrowhawk.

Treecreepers thrive in all kinds of woods, from pure deciduous to pure coniferous, natural or planted. Coal tits, however, prefer conifers and, especially in mixed woods, usually concentrate around a couple of old pines. Jays also live in all kinds of woods and seem to be particularly frequent in plantations of pine, but they are especially dependent on oak, as they gather vast numbers of acorns each autumn. Watch for them flying to and fro over such woods as they ferry loads of acorns and bury thousands for future use: they have a remarkable ability to remember where they put them.

▲ Nuthatches are able to come head first down a tree as easily as they climb up. They wedge the nuts and berries into crevices to hammer them open with their sharp bills.

▲ Crossbills are nomadic birds, settling wherever they can find a good crop of pine cones, which they prise open with their crossed beaks.

▶ Capercaillies need mature pine forest with plentiful berries. However, their future in Britain, where they are confined to Scotland, looks increasingly bleak.

Ancient conifer forest

With a good ground cover of bilberry and crowberry, this is ideal for a rare, giant, forest grouse, the capercaillie, while the black grouse prefers woodland edges and scattered trees spilling out over heather moors and rushy fields. In Europe the hazel grouse is another rare and elusive forest grouse. Europe has a range of woodpeckers and owls that live in forests, most tending to be rare, elusive or both. The UK has far fewer species and Ireland even fewer owls and no woodpeckers at all.

Conifer specialists

Conifers have special birds – crossbills. Three species breed in the UK: the common, the Scottish and the parrot. A fourth species, the two-barred crossbill, appears as a rare vagrant. All have specialized bills with crossed tips, for prising open cones to reach the seeds inside.

Another conifer specialist is the minute goldcrest. It is widely spread through mixed and sometimes deciduous woods, but reaches its greatest abundance in conifer woods, where it is one of the most characteristic songbirds. In summer, sunny clearings in many such woods form territories for spotted flycatchers.

▲ Hen harriers nest in plantations of small pines, but soon move out when the trees become too large. They have a more secure future on open moorland but are subject to frequent persecution.

Young conifer plantations

Young plantations of spruce and pine on heather moors are briefly good for short-eared owls, hen harriers and black grouse, but soon grow too large, dense and dark and have little but the common birds of mature conifer woods.

Where there are clearings and along the edges of these conifer plantations, tree pipits and whinchats arrive each spring. In the south of the UK and more widely in Europe, the open spaces around felled conifers and very young plantations, with some bare, sandy soil, attract woodlarks; and felled areas are also good for nightjars, which sing from isolated trees and hunt moths over open ground at dawn and dusk.

Heath and moor

Heathland is maintained by exposure to wind and frost, impoverished or very acid soils, waterlogging, heavy grazing, cutting and burning, or a mixture of several of these factors.

Lowland heaths

These are rare in most areas of Europe and are seen at their glorious best in parts of England, especially in Surrey, the New Forest and Dorset. East Anglia has similar heaths with an abundance of heather and gorse near the coast, but a different, grassy heath on sandy soils (the Brecks) inland. Maritime heaths above sea cliffs can be a riot of colour in summer, with dwarf heather and gorse predominating.

MUST KNOW

Heathland
This is characterized by an open aspect, with low growing herbs, grasses and sedges, and rushes and dwarf shrubs, but few or no trees. There are two main types:
● Southern or lowland heaths (including maritime heaths)
● Upland heaths (including similar habitats at lower altitudes further north).

◀ A typical heathland bird is the stonechat, which scolds intruders from the top of a bush, fence post or an overhead wire.

These heaths used to be grazed by sheep and cattle and were often burned and cut for 'furze' (gorse), all of which prevented tree growth, but many are now reverting to forest as such traditions have declined and the tree regeneration is unchecked. Tree growth brings in common woodland birds, but it removes the heathland specialists, including the woodlarks, nightjars, stonechats, linnets, meadow pipits and Dartford warblers, which, unusually for warblers, are resident in Britain and susceptible to bad winters. They sing from patches of tall heather and gorse in parts of the south.

▲ Linnets feed by standing on the ground and reaching up to pull seeds from short plants: they are not agile enough to feed in the tops of taller vegetation.

▼ Meadow pipits breed on moorland and some lower heaths but move to lowland farms and coastal marshes in winter, when the heaths are bleak and have little insect food to offer.

▶ The large-scale felling of mature conifer plantations has recently opened up much ground to woodlarks, which like open spaces with plenty of loose, sandy soil.

Lookout posts

Almost all the heaths' birds require a scattering of song or lookout posts, usually small trees, and open ground in which to feed. Stonechats perch on the very tops of gorse or heather stems, scolding intruders (including people), but will drop down to the ground to snatch up passing insects. Woodlarks sing from taller trees but usually in high, circling song flights from February or March onwards. Indeed, many people rate their rich, throaty warblings as among the best of all European bird songs.

▼ Merlins nest in the north and west but they move lower down from the hills in the winter months, visiting farmland and marshes in the south and east.

Heaths in winter

In winter, open heaths are visited by hunting hen harriers and merlins and perhaps a great grey shrike, which uses the scattered pines and birch trees as look-out posts as it hunts voles, mice and small birds. Most, however, are almost devoid of birds for several months, but where there are more trees, roaming flocks of redwings and fieldfares often come to roost each evening and some copses have large mixed roosts of crows and jackdaws.

Upland heaths

These are often boggy, rising from the edges of the valley-side farmlands to the high tops. Vast areas are poor grasslands on deep peat, where birds are few, with meadow pipits, skylarks and perhaps curlews most obvious in summer. Others have extensive heather, but too much burning or excessive grazing may reduce a heather moor to grass, with a consequent loss of birds, such as red grouse, black grouse, merlins, golden plovers, whinchats and stonechats. Nevertheless, in summer there is always a chance of a passing hen harrier or hunting short-eared owl, and kestrels are usually active.

▲ A predator on medium-sized birds, the peregrine is the largest of the UK's regular falcons. It breeds mostly near coastal cliffs and in moorland areas.

Mixed heather moors

Mixed heather moors with bracken and rushes in the valleys, grassy and mossy areas, and stony outcrops on the higher ridges are excellent for birds, with ravens, carrion or hooded crows, hen harriers, peregrines, buzzards, red kites, ring ouzels and wheatears all possible. Harriers nest in the long heather but often hunt over grassy ground where there are more pipits, larks and voles. Merlins may nest on the ground, or in old crows nests in isolated bushes, and hunt meadow pipits and large heathland moths.

An abundance of meadow pipits also attracts cuckoos, which lay eggs in the pipits' nests. Flocks of young starlings and rooks come to feed on insects in late summer. Reed buntings sing from damper patches in the valleys, where curlews often nest. Black-headed gulls nest beside peaty moorland pools, while common sandpipers and dippers can be found beside rushing upland streams.

In late summer, rowan berries in clumps of trees growing from sheltered gullies are eagerly taken by groups of mistle thrushes, sometimes joined by ring ouzels.

MUST KNOW

Twites
In fields beside the moors and in patches of heather, there may be twites, small relatives of the linnets of lowland heaths. Unusually among European birds, they require a constant supply of seeds in summer to feed their chicks, and the loss of traditional hay meadows has made life difficult for them in many areas.

Mountains

European mountains include spectacular ranges, such as the Alps and Pyrenees. Many of the birds found here can also be seen at much lower altitudes further north and west, where lower temperatures and greater exposure create similar conditions.

Highlands

Even within the UK, this effect can be seen. In the central Highlands, ptarmigan may be spotted at over about 2,500 feet above sea level, but in the far north can be encountered at less than half that altitude. In summer, the ptarmigan is a pepper-and-salt mixture of grey, black and white (females are much browner), while in spring and autumn it has more patches of white, and in winter becomes almost wholly white, except for its black tails. Such birds as the ptarmigan and the rarer snow bunting, however, are threatened by climatic change and are forced higher, or further north, if there is suitable habitat for them.

▼ Snow buntings are extremely rare breeders in Scotland, but are more widespread as winter visitors from the far north on hills, moors and coasts.

Golden eagles

In the UK, golden eagles are almost exclusively Scottish. They hunt over enormous areas of high ground, including open moors, screes, rolling, tundra-like high tops and rocky peaks, where they find a diet of ptarmigan, red grouse and mountain hares.

There are 430 pairs in Scotland but they can be frustratingly hard to see: spend some time scanning high peaks and distant skylines, as you are unlikely to get very close to one, but you do have a good chance to see a distant 'dot'. A close-up view of a big soaring bird is far more likely to be a buzzard and, if you see one sitting on a roadside fence post or telegraph pole, it will certainly be a buzzard, not an eagle. Buzzards are much less likely, however, to go over the highest, rockiest peaks.

▲ Only one pair of golden eagles has bred in England in recent years, and that may have come to an end with the loss of one of the adults. Numbers in Scotland have remained static, but an increase in the Western Isles seems to have balanced the losses to persecution elsewhere.

Ravens

These are exceptionally widespread birds in the northern hemisphere, ranging from the Arctic to hot deserts. They nest on cliff ledges and in big trees, laying very early when the weather is still harsh and often incubating their eggs during falls of snow. They are tough, dramatic birds, easily located if you know their loud, resonant, deep-throated call notes. As big as a buzzard, and with tricks of their own, such as rolling briefly upside down in flight, they are great birds to see.

▲ Ravens are massive, black crows, whose beautiful, resonant calls echo around cliffs and mountain peaks.

Other birds

Choughs and alpine choughs breed in southern European mountains, but in the UK the chough is not a mountain bird, preferring the vicinity of sea cliffs. Rock doves have been replaced in mountain areas by their 'gone wild' descendants, feral (or town) pigeons, but truly wild rock doves from coastal cliffs in north Scotland penetrate the moors inland on feeding forays.

▼ The chough breeds in the mountains of Europe and is a rare bird of UK coasts, feeding on beaches but more often on old pastures with plenty of insects.

Summer birds

A special wading bird comes to northern hills to breed in summer: the dotterel spends the winter in North Africa. A plover, it likes stony and grassy ridges at high altitude for nesting. Golden plovers also like high heathery ridges and open areas of limestone grassland, as well as lower heathery moors. They gather in flocks before and after nesting in crofters' fields at the moorland edges, and move to lowland farmland in winter.

Over UK mountain tops, in summer, black-headed gulls may be found foraging for insects and food left by climbers. Swifts drift overhead, feeding on airborne insects. In southern Europe, alpine swifts and crag martins may join them.

▲ Open hills with long, sweeping ridges and grassy plateaux are ideal for golden plovers in summer. Their plaintive calls seem ideally fitted to this wild, windswept environment.

MUST KNOW

Hill walking

This is an exhilarating pastime but most birds will be rather few and far between and some of the most exciting, such as the eagles, are likely to be seen only at long range. Never take moors, hills and mountains lightly: they can be dangerous places, where the weather is liable to change very quickly and catch out the unwary. You must follow good practice, such as using the right footwear and clothing, taking food and drink, good maps and a compass, and telling people where you are going and when you expect to get back.

Freshwater habitats

Rivers develop from the tiniest, clear upland stream to a broad watercourse, heavy with silt, approaching an estuary. Some major rivers reach complex deltas at the coast, but are mostly channelled into unchanging courses between steep embankments. Not many river stretches are left uncontrolled, and few floodplains remain unprotected from floods, as they are flooded naturally at times of heavy water flow.

Floodland

There are still areas of floodland, such as the washlands of East Anglia and the West Country. These were traditionally flooded in winter, attracting vast numbers of wildfowl (such as wigeons and Bewick's swans) and wading birds (including huge numbers of lapwings and snipe). They dried out in summer, when many species nested on their rich meadows, including snipe, redshanks, mallards and yellow wagtails.

Recently, however, a changing climate, increased building on floodplains and the large-scale drainage of many areas further upstream have tended to cause much flooding in spring, ruining the nesting seasons of thousands of birds in some years.

▼ Wigeon are rare breeders but common visitors to the UK marshes from autumn to spring. The males have distinctive yellow foreheads and short, blue-grey bills.

Wetlands

As well as rivers, there are wetlands of many different kinds – natural and artificial. Marshes and reedbeds have become rather rare and there are few opportunities for new areas to replace those that are lost to drainage and development. We have mentioned gravel pits (see page 140), but natural lakes share many of their attributes and are often better for wading birds, as they have shallower, muddier edges.

As many lakes have been drained, and innumerable farm ponds and small pools have been lost from the lowland landscape, so reservoirs have taken on a greater significance for wildlife. They also serve as centres for watery recreations for people, such as sailing and water skiing, which may conflict to a greater or lesser degree with the wildlife value. Some larger reservoirs cope by having nature reserves at one end and recreation zones at the other.

▲ The best reservoirs can be full of birds and great places for birdwatching.

MUST KNOW

Reservoirs

Reservoirs mimic natural lakes but have a greater tendency for dramatic changes in level: a rise in spring may flood out nesting birds, while a fall in late summer and autumn can create perfect conditions for migrant waders, seeking wet or dried mud on which to feed.

Upland lakes

These, together with reservoirs in deep upland valleys, tend to be different in character. They are often deeper, usually colder and typically acid, with little or no obvious vegetation at the edges, so they lack the breeding reed and sedge warblers, reed buntings, moorhens and coots.

Lowland lakes

Lowland lakes, especially reservoirs on farmland, are richer and less acid, but subject to sudden algal blooms at times, which soak up their oxygen and suffocate water plants and fish. While an upland lake may have little but a few common sandpipers and perhaps a pair or two of black-headed gulls in summer and the occasional goldeneye and mallard in winter, lowland ones can attract a host of birds in summer, including breeding yellow wagtails, reed and sedge warblers, kingfishers, mallards and tufted ducks, great crested grebes and cormorants, sand martins and reed buntings.

▲ Sedge warblers need rough, tangled vegetation near water and are birds of lowland lakes, not bleak, barren upland ones.

◄ Mallards can be found almost anywhere there is water, but they also fly to feed on fields at night, far away from their daytime wetland roost.

They have a vast number of migrants in spring and autumn, from swallows and martins over the water, chiffchaffs and other warblers in waterside bushes and pipits and buntings on the shores to dunlins, curlews, redshanks and many kinds of ducks. In winter they offer a wide array of wildfowl, such as goldeneyes, goosanders, wigeon, mallards, shovelers, gadwalls and teals and big flocks of roosting gulls.

Lowland reservoirs

Together with flooded gravel pits, these are some of the best places for birdwatching, especially away from the coast, as water always concentrates birds and adds such variety of habitat that there may be scores of species not found in ordinary farmland or woods. At the same time, most lakes and reservoirs will be close to farmland or woodland, anyway, and birds typical of those habitats can be seen nearby at the same time, virtually ensuring a good day out, at any time of year.

▲ Reed buntings are more often found in mixed sedges, reeds, reedmace and bushes than in pure reed.

▼ Gulls and lapwings rest in large numbers by reservoirs: gulls will move onto water at night for greater safety.

Coasts and islands

Europe has a massively long coastline, and that of the United Kingdom is exceptionally rich in coastal birds. Habitats vary from muddy estuaries and open sandy bays to sheer cliffs, but they all have great value for birds.

Estuarine environment

As a river reaches the sea, it widens and it will deposit its load of silt as mud in an estuary. Incoming tides swirl around the mouth of the estuary and build up a network of sand and shingle. Behind this a saltmarsh builds up: thick, rich mud dissected by innumerable creeks and overgrown with short, salt-tolerant plants. In some places there are sand dunes, stabilized by a thick growth of marram, with low-lying dune slacks just inland where shallow pools are rich in flowers and insect life.

▼ Grey plovers and smaller dunlins are great travellers, breeding right up in the Arctic, but relying on our estuaries for their survival in autumn and winter.

The whole complex of such an estuarine environment can be full of birds. In summer, the dunes are alive with singing larks and meadow pipits; stonechats and whinchats breed. The saltmarsh may have nesting redshanks, lapwings and curlews and colonies of black-headed gulls. Sandy beaches and shingle banks attract breeding common, Sandwich and little terns. The mouth of the estuary, with shingle, beds of mussels and offshore tide races is excellent for oystercatchers and eiders. Sea ducks, including scoters and long-tailed ducks, feed offshore on shellfish and crustaceans.

From autumn to spring the rich estuarine mud teems with waders, including bar-tailed and black-tailed godwits, grey plovers, dunlins, knots and redshanks. Brent geese, wigeon, mallards and other ducks graze the marsh plants and the eel grass and algae that grow on exposed mudflats. Gulls are everywhere here, scavenging on the marsh and the muddy beaches, or finding food brought to the surface in the offshore currents. They are equally common around fish quays, ferry terminals and promenades.

▲ Oystercatchers breed in the UK, but far larger numbers arrive here every autumn from further north. They feed in muddy, sandy, shingly and rocky places, taking shellfish of all kinds from a variety of habitats.

▼ Little terns nest on sand and shingle beaches: just the sort that people like, too. Disturbance and predation have caused a great decline in numbers and reduction in range.

MUST KNOW

Bays, beaches and headlands

Around the corner from an estuary, there may be bays with storm beaches of shingle and boulders, where turnstones turn over seaweed on the tideline to find food. Rocky headlands in winter are good for spotting purple sandpipers and oystercatchers.

Cliffs

Rocky islets and tumbling boulders in the north of the UK are good for arctic terns and black guillemots, which are rare or absent farther south. However, it is the seacliffs proper – sheer walls of rock above deep, surging sea – that are stunningly good for birds. In spring, huge numbers of fulmars, guillemots, razorbills, puffins and kittiwakes come to these cliffs to breed in noisy seabird cities. On one or two mainland cliffs and a handful of islands there are also gannets, in colonies of up to 40,000 pairs, the most spectacular of the North Atlantic seabirds.

▶ Vast colonies of seabirds on sheer coastal cliffs provide some of the most dramatic spectacles in our wildlife. Seabirds are among our finest treasures in the UK, in numbers that are internationally important.

Islands

Islands with screes and boulders, or deep earth riddled with burrows, are exciting places after dark, for this is when Manx shearwaters, and storm and Leach's petrels come to their nests. They are so ungainly on land, being made for life at sea, that they must avoid predatory gulls as far as possible. They are best seen from ships offshore or from headlands during spring and autumn, especially in periods of onshore winds that bring them in close.

In the northern islands, two species of skuas, great and arctic, breed on moors beside the cliffs. They are piratical and predatory and also fearless in defence of their nests: they will dive at the head of anyone who comes too close. Two other skuas, pomarine and long-tailed, pass by our coasts on the way to and from breeding areas in the Arctic.

▲ Unlike the guillemots and kittiwakes that nest on cliff ledges, Manx shearwaters nest in burrows. They are unable to walk on land and come to their nests only after dark, in an attempt to avoid predatory gulls that prey on them in summer.

Seawatching

In autumn, a headland such as Flamborough Head in Yorkshire can be a dramatic place if the conditions are right. Seabirds can move into the North Sea or the Irish Sea in large numbers. Blown close inshore by adverse winds, they then have to make their way out as best they can, sometimes coming by in a steady stream not far offshore. These include long-distance travellers, such as the sooty shearwaters that breed in the southern hemisphere and spend their 'winter' in the northern oceans. Sabine's gulls, birds of the far northern islands of the Canadian arctic, may pass by headlands on the west coast in north-westerly gales. Try 'seawatching' whenever you can: it is a special kind of birdwatching that is difficult but brings great rewards.

All in all, the coasts of north-west Europe are exceptional for birds of three main groups: the wildfowl (ducks, geese and swans), waders (plovers, sandpipers and their relatives) and seabirds, all of which can be found in their millions here.

▲ Cormorants are common seabirds, also seen inland.

▶ Oystercatchers are easily identified as they fly by on their migratory journeys.

▼ Great skuas are rare worldwide, with most of their breeding population in Scotland. They are bold predators and pirates.

Lagoons and reedbeds

Behind the low-lying coasts of much of southern and eastern Britain and large parts of the mainland European coast, shallow pools have formed, fringed with reeds and adjacent to wet grazing marshes. They are rich in wildlife, not least birds, but their species overlap with those found along softer, low-lying coasts, in estuaries and in freshwater marshes.

Reedbeds

Coastal reedbeds are generally bigger than any found inland and among the best for bitterns. Good reedbeds also have bearded tits, which live in no other habitat. These need more leaf-litter at the base of the reedbed than bitterns, for nesting in and in which to find insect food and fallen seeds. After good breeding seasons, numbers are so high that they 'erupt', moving off inland and exploring new reedbeds.

Breeding in the reeds will almost certainly be reed and sedge warblers. Cuckoos like these places because they can lay eggs in the nests of reed warblers. Other reedbed specialists include marsh harriers and, in rare instances, Montagu's harriers. Marsh harriers have greatly increased in Britain with recent protection and improvements in coastal reedbed habitat.

▲ Of all the specialist reedbed birds, bearded tits are perhaps the most beautiful and appealing. Their numbers have never been large, as they require extensive reedbeds in which to breed successfully.

MUST KNOW

Reedbeds in winter

In winter, the reedbeds attract birds that are not strictly marshland species, but which find good feeding here. Barn and short-eared owls hunt the fringes of the marsh and adjacent meadows. Blue tits are frequently found in parties in the reeds. And you may be startled more often than you expect by pheasants bursting up almost underfoot from the reedbed margins. Rarer birds appear occasionally, too, such as parties of Lapland buntings and shore larks on the edge of a marsh, while twites may mix with greenfinches, and snow buntings visit the seaward fringe.

Lagoons and backwaters

Where the reeds abut shallow pools, muddy
backwaters and lagoons, the birdwatching can
be exceptionally good. Nature reserves such as
Minsmere in Suffolk, and Titchwell Marsh and
Cley Marshes in Norfolk have wonderful varieties
of habitat in some small areas and consequently
exceptionally long lists of interesting birds to
watch. Minsmere has around 100 breeding
species, and Cley boasts a list of rarities that
beats any mainland site in England.

The pools are good for breeding waders,
including avocets, as well as large numbers of
migrants with regular black-tailed godwits, spotted
redshanks, little stints, curlew, wood sandpipers
and even scarcer waders – if a wader has
crossed the Atlantic from North America, this is
the kind of place it is most likely to be found.

Most frequent in Europe are pectoral and
white-rumped sandpipers, but you might be
lucky enough to hear about a greater rarity, such
as a long-billed dowitcher or a lesser yellowlegs.

▲ If you are lucky, you may
see a marsh harrier. These
birds are reed specialists,
nesting in the reeds, but
feeding over open ground
and water nearby.

Wildfowl

There are also breeding Canada and greylag geese, introduced into southern Britain, and wilder teals, mallards, shelducks and other ducks, supplemented each autumn by much bigger numbers of wildfowl from the north and east. Shelducks are bold, striking birds, easily seen at long range across the marsh.

▼ Wild greylag geese used to breed in southern Britain but were hunted to extinction. Reintroduced flocks are better than nothing, but much tamer.

▲ Black-headed gulls are seabirds for part of the year but many nest in marshy places well inland.

Seabirds

Breeding gulls may, in southern England, include increasing numbers of Mediterranean gulls, which are recent colonists in the UK. Another new arrival is the little egret, now commonly seen on coastal lagoons and estuaries around much of southern and eastern Britain and southern Ireland. Black-headed gull colonies tend to be large, hundreds or thousands strong on some coasts. You may also find groups of common, little and Sandwich terns nesting, although these tend to be fickle and subject to disturbance and predation.

While seabird colonies on cliffs can be watched in safety from viewpoints, colonies of terns are best avoided to reduce disturbance. An exception may be the colonies on the Farne Islands, where arctic terns are unusually bold and tame.

want to know more?

Take it to the next level...

Go to...
- ▶ **Getting involved** – page 178
- ▶ **Joining a club** – page 186
- ▶ **Need to know more?** – page 188

Other sources
- ▶ **Wetland Bird Survey (WeBS)**
  counting birds for conservation
- ▶ **Seabird 2000**
  for finding out more about seabirds
- ▶ **Internet**
  for information on conservation surveys
- ▶ **Birdwatching clubs**
  for meeting other birdwatchers
- ▶ **Publications**
  visit www.collins.co.uk for Collins bird books

getting

involved

Once you are set up as a birdwatcher, with a field guide, binoculars, and favourite places to visit, you might want to get more involved with other birdwatchers, a bird club or a conservation organization; it's up to you. Birdwatching has the great benefit of being the easiest, cheapest and least regulated pastime that you can possibly imagine.

Take it one step further

Birdwatching may be just an enjoyable hobby for you, and that's great if so. You may spend years enjoying garden birds and leave it at that. Birdwatching has no rules, and you should just enjoy it. Attracting birds to your garden is one way to develop your hobby that benefits the birds as well. However, you can take it further and give it a purpose.

Getting more out of it

Garden birds can give us a lifetime's enjoyment, but you might want to take your birdwatching a bit further, to get a little more out of it. Getting more out generally means putting more in, and there might be more paperwork and more correspondence. If you move into conservation matters, you might find yourself feeling angry, depressed or even helpless. Then again, you may get great satisfaction and joy out of winning a fight for the birds.

Rarely does the birdwatcher assess these things in advance. Birdwatching takes you into places you've never been in so many ways, like it or not. You may not be a campaigner until someone threatens to tear up the hedge across the road, or fill in the village pond, or build a motorway across your favourite fields. Then you go into battle. Good luck to you.

◀ The devastation of Twyford Down near Winchester, for a new road development, brought together many unexpected allies in an unsuccessful campaign to save it. You may have more impact in local campaigns to save valuable wildlife sites.

Extend your horizons

Not all birdwatchers wish to or, indeed, can afford to travel, but getting to a new habitat, such as the coast, is the simplest way to see more birds than you can observe close to home.

▲ Holidays open up a new world of birds. In much of southern and central Europe the hoopoe is one of the more exotic-looking species that you might never get a chance of seeing at home.

Holidays abroad

These offer huge opportunities for spotting new or unfamiliar birds, but you should always try to consider the environmental impact of your travel, especially if you have to fly to your holiday destination. Your first visit to southern Europe will be especially exciting, as this area is full of new, colourful birds and identification challenges. You may well find that you want to go again and again. If you are visiting somewhere for the first time, a good field guide, which is relevant to the birds of that particular area, is essential.

Holidays

Keep records of the
birds you see when
you are on holiday. **In
fact, holidays that are
taken in more remote
places, where there
are few birdwatchers
about, can add more
useful information
than a year spent in
a well-known area.**

▼ Records of birds such as
the tree sparrow and corn
bunting have become vitally
important as so many
farmland species are now
increasingly rare and
localized. Conservationists
need to know where they
can still be found.

Use your records

To start with, it's a good thing to make use of
your records: tell others what you see. If nothing
else, conservation relies on information. How
awful it would be if you knew of a great place for
birds then had no evidence to back up your
claims when it was about to be built on. Planners
and developers like to see designations – sites
of special scientific interest, special areas for
conservation, and areas of local or national
importance. If your marsh has not got any, it is
not going to get the protection it deserves. So
build up a record, and tell someone.

The best way is to send in your records to the
county or regional recorder. Find a name and
address from *The Birdwatcher's Yearbook* or
a website, or by contacting the BTO or RSPB
(see page 188). There is a network of voluntary
recorders who get thousands of reports every
year, file them, computerize them, and make
them into annual reports. These are vastly useful
to you, as you can read where and when birds
have been seen in your county, which helps you
see more yourself. In turn, your records help
build up the picture of the county birdlife.

Take part in surveys

Join the BTO or, if not, at least look at what they are doing and join in some surveys. If you are moderately competent and fit enough to walk a mile or two, you can do a Breeding Bird Survey, which helps monitor the ups and downs of our breeding birds year by year.

Such surveys have revealed the loss of such birds as skylarks, yellowhammers, tree sparrows and lapwings from much of our countryside, as well as the spread of more successful species. You have a part to play in this practical gathering of data, and it is a satisfying part. Now you can feel that you are putting something back, using your knowledge and doing something useful.

Simpler surveys

If not the BTO, then try the RSPB's generally simpler surveys, such as the annual Big Garden Birdwatch, in which more than 400,000 people participate, and also periodic surveys of various garden birds, house sparrows and the like. These allow practically anyone to get involved, just by looking out of the window. The BTO has a long-running garden bird survey, too, requiring a bit more application, week by week, but it is easy, fun and worthwhile to do.

Volunteer work

You might also like to volunteer to work for a conservation body, by contacting a Wildlife Trust, or the RSPB, or some other organization direct (see page 188). Volunteering does not always mean digging holes and carting logs about: for instance, you might meet and greet visitors to wildlife reserves; or monitor the flowers, insects or even the birds if you are lucky; or even work in an office, doing the filing, or advising on the computer systems, or the accounts, or whatever it is that you are good at.

▲ Surveys of birds such as the skylark are carried out somewhere every year. Many national surveys are run by the BTO, often organized by the network of local bird clubs. Your contribution can be important and invaluable to the growth of knowledge about our birds and their continued wellbeing.

MUST KNOW

Bird surveys
The RSPB runs its garden bird survey every January. There is also usually a spring bird survey relating to birds in gardens or woodland birds. Keep an eye out for details in the members' magazine or online on the RSPB website.

Your local patch

A great way to develop your birdwatching is to find a 'local patch'. This does not have to exclude birdwatching in other places; you can still get about as much as you like. However, if you have a place where you can pop down for half an hour before or after work, in your lunch break or after school, this can be a great boon. If you can get there at weekends and put in the hours then, too, you are really blessed.

Become an expert

Now you might become the local expert: the one person who knows more than anyone else about the birds of this special place. Keep notes, make sketch maps, write lists, take note of the flowers, the butterflies and the dragonflies. Send in your records and put the place on the birdwatching map.

Don't neglect well-known places that already seem well covered; they may not be. A reservoir or gravel pit may attract scores of birdwatchers, but it may not have a 'regular' who knows the place inside out. Why not become that regular? It could be very rewarding.

▼ If you watch birds as often as you can at a specific place, such as the local reservoir or lake, you can become 'the expert' on its bird life. Even if there is nothing rare, you will get great satisfaction from knowing all about the birds that can be seen.

Finding rarities

You may not see rarities. But if, after five years, you see a green woodpecker for the first time, you know how good that is – anything might become unusual and exciting. If you watch an area time after time, one day you really will find something genuinely unexpected and rare, and then you will discover how satisfying it is to find it yourself, instead of chasing after something you read about on your pager!

A rarity demands discipline. Watch it as long as you can. Take notes, describe it, draw it, photograph it and get others to see it. Get proof, evidence and corroboration. Send the notes to the bird recorder, who will send them on to the national rarities committee. Great!

▲ Don't ignore flocks of gulls: they might, one day, contain a rarer bird amongst the usual black-headed and herring gulls, such as a glaucous gull or this Mediterranean gull. They are beautiful to look at, too.

Joining a club

There are scores of bird clubs all over the UK, from tiny ones that concentrate on one wetland, one nature reserve or even a 10 km square in the national grid, to big ones, such as the West Midland Bird Club, one of the oldest and biggest, that covers four counties. Join the club. You can get details from the RSPB, BTO or a local library. Many have websites now.

The benefits

Once you join you will probably get regular newsletters and (perhaps for an extra fee) an annual report. There will be regular outings that you can join and indoor meetings to attend. Here you can learn more about birds, places to watch birds, and people who see them. Birdwatching is often a lonely pursuit, best done quietly, with minimum disturbance. However, being excited by birds is best enjoyed with a companion. Nothing beats turning round to say 'Did you see that?' with feeling. Turning round, elated by a magnificent sight, to find no one there can be deflating.

So, if you want a birdwatching friend, join a club. If you just want to talk about birds, join a club. You will learn a lot, or you may teach a lot. Share experiences, ask questions, talk birds and birdwatching. It all helps to develop your hobby take you into new areas – photography, bird ringing, lecturing, writing or finding new books.

National societies

As well as local or county clubs, there are also national ones. There are societies covering Northern Ireland, Scotland and Wales, but not an English bird club. Until recently, there had not been an English bird book, although there are several on the other countries' birds. But there are UK-wide societies with their individual slants.

The RSPB

The RSPB (the Royal Society for the Protection of Birds) has more than a million members, doing the work of bird conservation, running more than 180 nature reserves (most of which you can visit), offering a quarterly magazine and running local groups, annual weekends and reserve events. It is a huge conservation operation, with lobbying, campaigning and involvement in local planning and scientific research.

The BTO

The BTO (British Trust for Ornithology) is a focus for voluntary work on all kinds of surveys, from regular ones, such as the Breeding Bird Survey, to censuses of particular species. It is the club for practical birdwatchers who want to add to the national data bank of birds in the UK. It also runs the ringing scheme, with licensed ringers catching, marking and releasing birds, so that recoveries of their rings can tell us about numbers, distribution, migrations and survival rates. The Nest Record Scheme monitors the breeding success of our birds, as well as changes in laying dates.

The Wildfowl & Wetlands Trust

This runs reserves and wetland centres and does research and conservation work focusing on ducks, swans and geese and their watery habitats around the world. Uniquely among big UK bird conservation organizations, it also has captive birds in large, ornamental (and also scientifically valuable) collections.

The Wildlife Trusts

These operate at county level, or in groups of counties, under a national banner. They promote local conservation, run nature reserves and produce local and national magazines.

▲ The headquarters of the RSPB are at Sandy in Bedfordshire. It is involved in valuable conservation work and scientific research.

GETTING INVOLVED

187

► # Need to know more?

A wealth of further information is available for birdwatchers, particularly if you have access to the internet. Listed below are some useful organizations and resources.

National societies
BirdLife International
Wellbrook Court, Girton Road,
Cambridge CB3 0NA
tel: 01223 277318
website: www.birdlife.net
The BTO (British Trust for Ornithology)
The Nunnery, Thetford, Norfolk IP24 2PU
tel: 01842 750050
e-mail: info@bto.org
website: www.bto.org
County bird clubs
The whole of the UK is covered by local or county bird clubs. For details, ask the RSPB or BTO or look at *The Birdwatcher's Yearbook.*
The RSPB (Royal Society for the Protection of Birds)
UK Headquarters, The Lodge, Sandy,
Bedfordshire SG19 2DL
tel: 01767 680551
e-mail: enquiries@rspb.org.uk
website: www.rspb.org.uk
Scottish Ornithologists Club
tel: 0131 653 0653
website: www.the-soc.fsnet.co.uk
Welsh Ornithological Society
www.welshornithologicalsociety.org.uk
The Wildfowl & Wetlands Trust
UK Headquarters, Slimbridge,
Gloucestershire GL2 7BT
tel: 01453 891900
e-mail: enquiries@wwt.org.uk
website: www.wwt.org.uk
The Wildlife Trusts
The Kiln, Waterside, Mather Road,
Newark, Nottinghamshire NG24 1WT
tel: 0870 036 7711
e-mail: enquiry@wildlife-trusts.cix.co.uk
website: www.wildlifetrusts.org.uk

Book, video, CD, DVD sales
BirdGuides
tel: 0800 919391
website: www.birdguides.com
Christopher Helm
tel: 01256 302692
website: www.acblack.com

HarperCollins Publishers
77–85 Fulham Palace Road
London W6 8JB
website: www.collins.co.uk
NHBS (Natural History Book Service)
2–3 Wills Road, Totnes,
Devon TQ9 5XN
tel: 01803 865913
website: www.nhbs.com
Wildsounds
tel: 01263 741100
website: www.wildsounds.co.uk

Rare birds
Rare Bird Alert
tel: 01603 456789
website: www.rarebirdalert.com
Rare bird news by mobile phone, pagers and website.

Binocular and telescope sales/digiscoping
Focus Optics
tel: 01676 540501
In Focus
tel: 01727 827799
website: www.infocusoptics.co.uk
Kay Optical
tel: 020 8648 8822
website: www.kayoptical.co.uk
LCE
tel: 01962 866203
website: www.digiscoping.co.uk
Leica
tel: 01908 246300
website: www.leica-camera.co.uk
Opticron
tel: 01582 726522
website: www.opticron.co.uk
RSPB Optics
tel: 01767 680541
website: www.rspboptics.com
Swarovski
tel: 01737 856812
website: www.swarovskioptik.com
Viking Optics
tel: 01986 875315
website: www.vikingoptical.co.uk

Zeiss
tel: 01707 871350
website: www.zeiss.co.uk

Birdwatching holidays
Birdfinders
tel: 01258 839066
website: www.birdfinders.co.uk
Birdquest
tel: 01254 826317
website: www.birdquest.co.uk
Honeyguide
tel: 01603 300552
website: www.honeyguide.co.uk
Limosa
tel: 01263 578143
website: www.limosaholidays.co.uk
Naturetrek
tel: 01962 733051
website: www.naturetrek.co.uk
Ornitholidays
tel: 01794 519445
website: www.ornitholidays.co.uk
Wildwings
tel: 0117 9375 689
website: www.wildwings.co.uk

Bird food and feeders, garden bird equipment
BoxWatch
(camera inside nestbox)
tel: 01342 850259
tel: 01484 720220
C.J. WildBird Foods Ltd
The Rea, Upton Magna,
Shrewsbury SY4 4UR
tel: 0800 731 2820
website: www.birdfood.co.uk
J.E. Haith Ltd
65 Park Street, Cleethorpes,
North East Lincolnshire DN35 7NF
tel: 0800 298 7054
website: www.haiths.com
Jacobi Jayne
tel: 0800 072 0130
website: www.jacobijayne.com
Nestview
(camera inside nestbox)
tel: 01900 872880
RSPB Online Store
tel: 0870 112 5421
website: www.rspbshop.co.uk
Soar Mill Seeds
tel: 0870 429 6195
website: www.soarmillseeds.co.uk
Vine House Farm
tel: 01775 630208
website: www.vinehousefarm.co.uk

Maps
Ordnance Survey maps
These can be obtained from most good newsagents, motorway services shops, etc. Or you can get information and view the maps online.
website: www.ordnancesurvey.co.uk/oswebsite/getamap

Bibliography

Barnes, Simon, *How to Be a Bad Birdwatcher* (Short Books)
Collins Gem: Birds (Collins)
Couzens, Dominic, *Birds by Behaviour* (Collins)
Couzens, Dominic, *Birds of Britain & Ireland* (Collins)
Flegg, Jim, *Time to Fly - Exploring Bird Migration* (BTO)
Hayman, Peter, and Rob Hume, *The Complete Guide to the Birds of Britain & Europe* (Mitchell Beazley)
Hayman, Peter, and Rob Hume, *The New Birdwatcher's Pocket Guide to Britain and Europe* (Mitchell Beazley)
Heinzel, Hermann, Richard Fitter and John Parslow, *Collins Pocket Guide: Birds of Britain and Europe* (Collins)
Holden, Peter, *Collins Wild Guide: Birds* (Collins)
Hume, Rob, *RSPB Birds of Britain and Europe* (Dorling Kindersley)
Jonsson, Lars, *Birds of Europe* (Christopher Helm)
Moss, Steven, *A Bird in the Bush - a social history of birdwatching* (Aurum)
Peterson, Roger T., Guy Mountfort and P.A.D. Hollom, *Collins Field Guide: Birds of Britain and Europe* (Collins)
RSPB, *The Complete RSPB Birds of Britain and Europe* (Collins)
Sample, Geoff, *Garden Bird Songs and Calls* (Collins)
Sterry, Paul, *Complete British Birds* (Collins)
Svensson, Lars, and Peter J. Grant, illustrated by Killian Mullarney and Dan Zetterström, *Collins Bird Guide* (Collins)
Tipling, David, *Top Birding Spots in Britain & Ireland* (Collins)

NEED TO KNOW MORE?

189

Glossary of terms

Bill: The same as beak – an extension of the jaws with a horny sheath.

Breeding plumage: The brightest plumage at a time when birds display, find mates and defend a territory.

Breeding season: The period of the year when birds nest, lay eggs and rear their young.

Brood: A set of young birds reared at one time, from one clutch of eggs.

Clutch: A set of eggs incubated by a sitting bird.

Colony: A group of nests close together.

Flock: A group of birds, acting to some extent in concert.

Habitat: The characteristics of a bird's environment, including the flora and fauna, soils, water, climate and altitude.

Incubation: Maintaining even temperature of an egg, by sitting (brooding), so the embryo develops and hatches.

Migration: Regular seasonal movement of bird populations.

Nest: A receptacle for eggs and, in some cases, chicks.

Pair: A male and female, together for the purpose of breeding – a basic unit used in counting the numbers of birds.

Passage migrant: A bird that neither breeds nor winters in an area but may be seen in spring and autumn.

Plumage: The covering of feathers. Also different age, season or sexual variations in appearance of plumage.

Preening: Caring for the feathers by drawing each one through the bill to maintain its shape and structure; also to add oil from the preen gland to keep the feathers waterproof.

Roost: To sleep; a place where a bird sleeps; a group of birds sleeping or resting together.

Territory: An area of ground defended by one bird, or a pair, or a family group, against others of the same species for the purpose of nesting (and providing food) or, outside the breeding season, for feeding.

Vocalization: A 'call' (or call note), used for keeping contact, warning of predators, begging for food; or a 'song', used by males (sometimes females) to help proclaim and defend a territory and attract a mate.

Acknowledgements

Photographs are reproduced courtesy of rspb-images.com: Steve Austin: pp. 74, 138, 171; Niall Benvie: back cover (bottom) and pp. 48, 79, 90, 100; Nigel Blake: pp. 75, 102, 113, 153, 156; David Broadbent: pp. 21, 178; Richard Brooks: pp. 55, 103, 104, 130, 148, 170, 175; Peter Cairns: pp. 62, 108; Laurie Campbell: pp. 38, 70, 92, 114; Colin Carver: p. 141; Paul Doherty: pp. 50, 99; Geoff Dore: p. 131; Gerald Downey: pp. 90, 126, 133, 164; John Farmar: p. 111; Bob Glover: back cover (centre) and pp. 40, 54, 66, 81, 86, 103, 157, 176, 183; Chris Gomersall: pp. 2, 3, 33, 34, 35, 41, 42, 44, 56, 71, 79, 86, 108, 112, 113, 122, 135, 139, 140, 141, 144, 147, 167, 169, 177, 180; Michael Gore: p. 49; Jan Halady: p. 1; Mark Hamblin: back cover (top) and pp. 3, 17, 60, 77, 87, 118, 120, 145, 159, 161, 182; Tony Hamblin: pp. 36, 56, 57, 75, 78, 121, 128, 152; Andy Hay: pp. 14, 20, 22, 23, 30, 37, 57, 91, 95, 107, 116, 125, 135, 146, 162, 168, 187; Robert Horne: pp. 169, 184; Barry Hughes: p. 67; Malcolm Hunt: front cover and pp. 15, 18, 63, 128, 142, 157; Ernie Janes: pp. 32, 46, 51, 94, 124, 165; Ray Kennedy: pp. 76, 80, 105, 111, 132, 140; David Kjaer: pp. 19, 150; Steve Knell: pp. 8, 72, 81, 154, 158, 160; Chris Knights: pp. 25, 65, 68, 69, 85, 89, 93, 115, 119, 138, 149, 154; Mike Lane: pp. 61, 77, 96, 114, 119, 143, 163, 166, 167, 172, 181, 185; Gordon Langsbury: pp. 58, 59, 82, 131, 142, 173; Genevieve Leaper: p. 137; George McCarthy: pp. 12, 96, 98, 105, 106, 109; Mike McKavett: p. 158; Phillip Newman: pp. 52, 155; Bill Paton: pp. 84, 85, 133, 136, 137; rspb-images.com: pp. 37, 64, 129; Mike Read: pp. 7, 27, 151; Richard Revels: pp. 53, 142; Mike Richards: pp. 88, 96, 174; Roger Tidman: p. 101; David Tipling: pp. 2, 38, 121, 129; Maurice Walker: p. 11; Roger Wilmshurst: pp. 97, 107, 110

Index